Theology and Eschatology
At the Turn of the Millennium

Edited by

James J. Buckley
and

L. Gregory Jones

Copyright © Blackwell Publishers Ltd 2001

First published as vol. 16, issue 1 of *Directions in Modern Theology*, 2000

Blackwell Publishers Ltd
108 Cowley Road, Oxford OX4 1JF, UK

Blackwell Publishers Inc
350 Main Street,
Malden, Massachusetts 02148, USA

British Library Cataloguing in Publication Data

A CIP catalogue record for this book is available from
the British Library

Library of Congress Cataloging-in-Publication Data has been applied for

ISBN 0-631-23395-4

Typeset in Great Britain
by Advance Typesetting

This book is printed on acid-free paper

MIX
Paper from
responsible sources
FSC   FSC® C013604
www.fsc.org

CONTENTS

INTRODUCTION

"Eschatology" has been crucial for modern theology. We suspect that the new millennium will yield some ruminations on this topic. But, if these ruminations are to become theological, it is important to remember that eschatology has not been important in some single way. Jewish and Christian apocalyptic, traditional beliefs about resurrection of the body and eternal life, re-readings of medieval millenarian movements, competing modern and postmodern utopias and futurologies as well as ideologies of despair and violence—all of these make a claim on modern theology's eschatology, but in different and competing ways. Our goal in this volume is to bring together students of Scripture, the history of Christianity, and various contemporary theologies so that readers can think about and debate the ways diverse and often conflicting eschatological narratives, images, and beliefs might bear on the millennium.

This issue of *Modern Theology* will also be a volume in the Directions in Modern Theology series.[1] As is also the case with other volumes, the essays here aim both to describe and to give "directions in modern theology". But they make no claim to systematic completeness and can be read in different orders than the one we have chosen. David Aers offers a reading of William Langland's fourteenth century Christian poem, *Piers Plowman*, as an engagement with competing millenarian (neo-Joachite) and Augustinian eschatological traditions within the late medieval Church. Langland's poem offers critique, political and ecclesial. The critique is at once trinitarian and christological, and therefore Piers "stays in the Church despite its infiltration by the forces of Antichrist". Paul Griffiths proposes a syntax for concerns with eschatology as various sorts of endings of temporal sequences, and for Christian eschatology as endings of a particular narratable history. Christians represent eternal life beyond this narrative completion apophatically as well as iconically. Used like Israel used Egyptian gold, Nirvana can become a Christian icon of the end. Amy Plantinga Pauw reflects on angels and devils as living out the eschatological ends of glory or damnation, using Jonathan Edwards and Karl Barth as test cases. But the place of angels and demons in theology is analogous to the practice of Baroque musical ornamentation. They are not the main melody but enhance other theological themes, leaving considerable room for theological freedom and innovation—particularly the freedom to defer to those who delight in ornamenting the main themes of God in Christ.

Sarah Coakley finds cultural contradictions in our obsessions with a body at once sexually affirmed and disciplined with diet and exercise. But such contradictions hide a latent yearning for an elusive eschatological goal. Judith Butler and Gregory of Nyssa are brought into dialogue and debate on precisely this issue: gender fluidity is a parable of ascetical transformation rather than anarchistic politics. David Ford points out that Christian eschatology has traditionally been lived and thought in supercessionist fashion with regard to the Jewish people. Using a pragmatic hermeneutic on the Epistle to the Ephesians, David Ford proposes a non-supercessionist Christ —the face of a Christ before whom we ourselves face "the double testimony of Golgotha and Auschwitz". Miroslav Volf recovers a social dimension of eschatology, suggesting a final reconciliation as a transformation of the existing world of enmity into a world of love rather than a final judgment creating a brand new world of love for individuals. This final reconciliation is begun and sustained by God's grace and participated in by sinful persons, "the Triune God moving toward sinful humanity to take them up into the circle of divine communal love". Richard Hays discusses three unsatisfactory strategies of dealing with Ernst Käsemann's maxim that "apocalyptic is the mother of Christian theology" before proposing one of his own. Debates among students of the New Testament on our topic are as intense as any, and readers might wonder how the other authors would address the issues Hays and his colleagues are debating.

This, of course, would be the next step that this volume does not take: debate among us over how these diverse uses of eschatology can make the millennium a parable of more significant, and holy, endings.

NOTES

1 L. Gregory Jones and Stephen E. Fowl, eds., *Rethinking Metaphysics* (Blackwells, 1995); L. Gregory Jones and James J. Buckley, eds., *Spirituality and Social Embodiment* (Blackwells, 1997); L. Gregory Jones and James J. Buckley, eds., *Theology and Scriptural Imagination* (Blackwells, 1998); Sarah Beckwith, ed., *Catholicism and Catholicity* (Blackwells, 1999).

CHAPTER 1
VISIONARY ESCHATOLOGY: *PIERS PLOWMAN*

DAVID AERS

"The believer, and thus the *community* of belief, is charged with actualizing in any and every circumstance the Easter transaction, the Easter restoration. There is no alibi for the Church" (Rowan Williams, *Resurrection*).[1]

I

William Langland's *Piers Plowman* was written and rewritten from the 1360s through the 1380s and now exists in at least three identifiable versions.[2] In its B and C versions it is among the greatest of Christian poems. Only largely unexamined disciplinary constitutions estrange it from departments of theology and schools of divinity. This essay can only hope to begin questioning these constitutions for it inevitably abstracts a few strands and moments from an extremely long, dialogic poem of astonishing formal, theological, and political complexity, an allegorical vision whose procedures make it impossible to postulate individuals and their spirituality independently of the polities and narratives within which they have life as determinate human beings.

Langland wrote after the Black Death that killed over forty percent of the people in England. This human catastrophe, followed by further outbreaks of plague, unfolded in social and economic forms that included unprecedented opportunities for wage-laborers and peasants with substantial holdings to improve their material circumstances, opportunities resisted by the gentry and ecclesiastical hierarchy. Out of increasingly sharp struggles over wages, taxation, villein services, and law emerged the great English rising of 1381, one in which some rebels seem to have used *Piers Plowman*, a poem severely critical of contemporary law and the administration of justice. During the

David Aers
Duke University Divinity School, Durham, NC 27708, USA

rising the rebels who gained temporary control of London ceremoniously executed the Archbishop of Canterbury who was, symptomatically, Chancellor of England.[3] But the Church was confronting more than this episode. Langland wrote in a time of extraordinary divisions in the Church. From 1378 there were two popes given to organizing crusades against each other (organization that included the use of indulgences to raise funds), activity that John Wyclif took as a probable sign of the triumph of Antichrist in the last time. Simultaneously, the Church in England was encountering a movement of radical criticism directed against many of its practices and doctrines, including its resistance to the vernacularization of Scripture and theology. This tendency, Wycliffism or Lollardy, moved beyond the Latinate world of Oxford into the vernacular across England, and by 1401 agreement between the usurping Lancastrian dynasty (founded on the violent deposition of Richard II), parliament and the Church enabled the enactment of legislation long sought for by the Church: the penalty of death by burning for Christians who would not renounce their support for Wycliffite teachings.[4]

Given this essay's concentration on Langland's reflections and narratives *de novissimis*, we should note that his engagement with his world was simultaneously an engagement with diverse eschatological traditions within the late medieval Church. Among these, he was aware of millenarian, probably neo-Joachite, strands. Some modern readings have tried to assimilate *Piers Plowman* to these strands, while others have argued that Langland's eschatology is unambiguously Augustinian.[5] Langland's devotedly Christocentric vision together with his commitment to traditional allegorical exegesis and its theology gives us no good reason to pursue these conflicts here, or anywhere.[6] However, it is worth briefly recalling some of the distinctive features of Joachite eschatology as it was elaborated in the thirteenth and fourteenth centuries, especially by Spiritual Franciscans, for against these tendencies Langland set his face. Joachite eschatology involved a major rupture with traditional forms of allegorical exegesis, as Henri de Lubac demonstrated in detail, a radical break with the hitherto hegemonic Augustinian understanding of the millennium and Apocalypse 20. For Augustine, the millennium is the first resurrection of the dead; through Christ's Incarnation, Christians are raised to life in the Church while Christ has restrained Satan's powers over his people.[7] In Joachite traditions the millennium is relocated as the third *status* of salvation history, now unfolding, the era of the Holy Spirit to be fulfilled on earth after the defeat of the first Antichrist, an imminent historical event. This blissful *status* will see a transformed Church, consisting of spirituals and contemplatives.[8] Christ's Gospel needed and would receive completion within history. By the time Langland was writing another potential of Joachite tradition was emerging: its convergence with the rhetoric and forms of nationalism.[9]

Finally, we should remember that late medieval resources for thinking about millennium and eschatology also included St. Thomas's careful critiques of Joachite theologies of history, including their appropriation by anti-fraternal polemicists. In *Contra Impugnantes Dei Cultum Et Religionem,* St. Thomas draws on many New Testament texts to argue that the last days (*novissimi dies*) in which all Christians live have been correctly identified by Augustine and that the prophecy of Joel 2:28 has been decisively fulfilled at Pentecost (Acts 2:1–3). As for the end of history, he emphasizes Christ's insistence that it is not for his disciples to know the times (Acts 1:7).[10] Later, in the *Summa Theologiae,* he develops a critique of Joachim's treatment of the New Law and its alleged relation to a forthcoming era of the Holy Spirit. No *status* will supersede the New Law revealed in Christ's work and the Gospel: "no state [*status*] of our present life can be more perfect than the state of the New Law ... there can be no more perfect state of our life than the state of the New Law." Once again he maintains that the Holy Spirit was abundantly poured forth at Pentecost (Acts 2), fulfilling Christ's own promise (Acts 1:5). Any claim that "we should look forward to some new time of the Holy Spirit" is to be rejected as empty. Furthermore, the New Law belongs to Christ *and* the Holy Spirit. Finally, "since Christ began his preaching of the Gospel by saying *The kingdom of heaven is at hand* [Matt. 4:17], it is absurd [*stultissimum*] to say that the gospel of Christ is not the gospel of the kingdom."[11] With these words we can turn to Langland's poem.

II

Piers Plowman begins with Will, the figure of the poet (William Langland), and of the will (the rational appetite). He is following a mobile, ambivalent kind of life that is severely condemned in the poem which is his vision. It opens as a representation of later fourteenth century England, its people, preoccupations, practices, and major institutions set between a castle on a hill (heaven) and a dungeon in a valley (hell). The prologue shows the Church assimilated to contemporary markets and competition for wealth. Biblical exegesis is determined by material interests; simony is pervasive; the sacrament of penance is sold (the use of indulgences is presented as symptomatic of such commodification); and those vowed to follow the poor Christ, the friars, have become partisans and confessors of the powerful. The Church belongs to a polity figured forth through mice, rats, and a predatory cat (the lay sovereign). The outcome here is a society eerily akin to a Hobbesian model in which competitive violence is taken as foundational, an unalterable given to be contained by a sovereign to whom all power has been surrendered. Christian discipleship has been driven into the margins of a Christian polity that seems only vestigially Christian.[12] A woman comes down from the castle to address Will, who fails to recognize her. She is Holy Church. Lamenting people's total absorption into the "maze" and offering a powerful vision of nature and human fulfillment shaped by the Trinity and the Incarnation, she rejects any antithesizing of *recta ratio* and *fides,* of nature and grace, of individual and common good, of our natural and supernatural ends. Her puzzlement is that baptized Christians are apparently unable to recognize her or to grasp that their energetic pursuits in the "maze" have actually occluded the eschatological nature of reality (I.1–26, 46–78, 85–104, 130–137, 148–209). She then vanishes, leaving the poet to enter the maze of contemporary England and its conflicts, ones that involve a host of complex political, ethical, and theological issues.[13]

Much in the first three quarters of the poem can be seen, in a brutal reduction, as the poet's search for the resources of reformation in the polity and the Church. It is a search that resists attempts to generate a "spirituality" abstracted from embodied practices of the virtues and vices, or abstracted from the specific ways in which the Church is administering the sacraments. Gradually the vision reveals a remarkable absence of such resources in the contemporary Church's priesthood and regular orders since these are represented as having become assimilated to the "maze" and its version of human ends. Conscience and Reason struggle to reform the administration of justice, while Reason calls for repentance and confession (III–V), but the most promising force for transformations the poet desires is an agricultural laborer, a vernacular guide to the Christian virtues, Piers the Plowman, layman. His attempts to overcome social conflicts and struggles around the Statute of Laborers fail, but this leads to a conversion in which he proclaims the pursuit of a life shaped by Jesus's teaching on the mountain and the plain, an act of faith derisively opposed by a priest.[14] Under this challenge from the Church's clergy, Piers disappears for the next eight passus, a haunting memory and a source of many puzzles. His absence returns the reader to the situation in which even penitents blunder around with no guide who knows the way through the maze (V.510–536, VII.115–206). How does one go on in such a situation?

One way that may seem plausible when the Church's language of new life, reform, hope, and transformation seems to be horribly frustrated by various forms of wickedness is a turn to millenarian eschatology. The poet (as suggested in part one of this essay) was well aware of this potential in his culture and explores it. In the third passus Conscience attempts to reform a polity pervaded by market relations in which everything, including the sacrament of penance, is a commodity, a polity in which traditional distinctions between just and unjust prices are extremely difficult to maintain. His attempts are blocked and his frustration explodes in an invocation of 1 Kings [Samuel] 15–16 and Isaiah 2:2–5. Exultantly he declares that just as Agog was butchered by Samuel so shall contemporary opponents of his reforms be dealt with: a new David will become world ruler and one Christian king look after us all ("oon cristene kyng kepen vs echone", III.289), thus guaranteeing that the rule of money and unjust powers will finally end. Love and Conscience will effect a revolutionary transformation of ecclesiastic, legal, and political institutions. Any who resist this millennial peace, when swords are beaten into plowshares, will be executed. In this state the Jews will rejoice that Moses or Messiah has come, the time prophesied in Isaiah 2:2–5, a text "read at matins in the first week of Advent".[15] The millennial kingdom is, of course, to be preceded by what Conscience describes as the "worste" time (III.259–330).

This is one of the passages that has elicited most discussion among those seeking to assess the poet's relation to Joachite eschatology and millenarianism.[16] It certainly exhibits a millenarian eschatology that could have been stimulated by Joachite traditions, although non-Joachite apocalypticism was hardly rare in the later Middle Ages. But the passage has been carefully *placed* by the poet. Langland shows that this millenarian turn is grounded in the speaker's anger at the continual resistance to his projects of reformation. His apocalyptic mode generates the un-Augustinian expectation of an imminent eschatological peace within history, one governed by the kind of Christian world emperor ("oon cristene kyng") whom Jean de Roquetaillade expected to come from the kings of France.[17] The promise of such a Christian ruler dissolves the Christocentric liturgical contexts of Isaiah 2:2–5, as does the retention of the death penalty to punish transgressors against peace (III.286, 305–308, 324). The millenarian eschatology here is shown to have displaced the Word made flesh, crucified and resurrected, displaced the work of Christ, displaced the Church (within which Will is searching). In these crucial displacements it sets aside the humanity of Christ, the model of Christian virtues; and it forgets the distinctly Christian sources of the virtue patience. However remote Joachim's eschatology from versions cultivated by later admirers like Gerardo of Borgo San Domino or Jean de Roquetaillade, it compromised, in Henri de Lubac's words, "la pleine suffisance de Jésus-Christ".[18] It is such tendencies within medieval eschatology that Langland is exploring in the passage we have been reading. By ascribing it to Conscience he links such millenarianism with a reforming zeal whose longings and frustrations his poem embodies. But as St. Thomas too had taught, Conscience is not infallible and here his mistake lies in the displacements I have just identified.[19] *Piers Plowman* is teaching its readers to understand this kind of eschatology and its apocalyptic idiom *as a temptation*: however plausible and righteous its agents, Langland represents it as contributing to a displacement of the unsurpassable revelation of God's kingdom in the life, death, and resurrection of Jesus Christ.

How does *Piers Plowman* dramatize an appropriately Christocentric approach to eschatology? Langland's way through the "maze" is through Piers, the aging Will, the liturgy (especially from Lent to Pentecost), and a final return to the contemporary Church and world, from which the poem set out, so long ago. On this journey the poet deploys a wide range of narrative, allegorical, and disputational modes, organized with remarkable subtlety and theologic intelligence. We can follow some strands and moments.

Will's long and troubled education leads him to the kind of patient poverty to which Piers the Plowman had been converted, but he also has to hear a sustained critique of the contemporary Church from an authoritative figure (XV.80–148, 347–360, 444–573). Still longing for Charity, he is told that he will discover this virtue by attending to Piers, mysteriously glossed as Christ ("*Petrus id est Christus*") and by concentration on the stories of the saints following Christ's life (XV.149–306). This does not satisfy him (XVI.3), and the next stages of the poem are an extraordinary response to Will's search. He is first given a vision of charity as an allegorical tree growing in a garden called the heart under the supervision of Piers the Plowman and Liberum Arbitrium enabled by the presence of the Trinity (XVI.1–52).[20] Overwhelmed with joy at the very name of Piers, Will falls into a love-dream (XVI.18–20). Longing for the fruit of charity, he asks Piers if he might *taste* the desired fruit, apparently apples (XVI.73). Here commentators habitually moralize against Will, judging him to be reenacting the false move in Eden.[21] But such a judgment is wide of the mark and an impediment to grasping this resonant moment. Far from seeking autonomy in a denial of God, Will acts under the guidance of Piers, mysteriously, as yet, *Petrus id est Christus*. His desire, though he does not yet understand its meanings, is both memorial and eschatological. We should focus on his unprecedented joy, his fainting with love of Piers, and the longing to taste the "sauour" (XVI.74 a pun: savor/Savior). If we need a Scriptural analogue we should turn to the Song of Songs, a major resource for figuring the love of Christ in devotional writing and art of many kinds.[22]

There the bride celebrates her beloved "as an apple tree" whose shadow she has longed for and under which she is now seated, his fruit sweet to her taste (2:3). She desires to be encompassed with apples because she languishes with love (2:5; see also 5:8 and 8:5). Such is Will's state here. But commenting on these verses St. Bernard observes that the whole scene also recalls that despite the banquet promised by Christ, the tree of life, we are still "in the shadow as long as we walk by faith and not by sight". Living by faith in the shadow is living in the memory and sacraments of the humanity of Christ, the only way to the light whose fulfillment is eschatological.[23] St. Bernard's comments may help readers see why, when Piers pulls down the fruit Will justly yearns for, the apples are snatched away by the devil as they are transformed into human beings from Adam to John the Baptist (XVI.75–85). Will's longing, even if he does not yet realize this, is for Christ and the eschatological banquet. Piers's response sparks off the first in a sequence of narratives centered on the life, death, and resurrection of Christ, which shapes passus XVI–XIX (here, XVI.86–166). Only through the divine embracing of time is the accumulation of human suffering and destructiveness redeemable, and only in faith can those under the shadow of the apple tree grasp that historical time has been created as the merciful gift of God. And this is only graspable, so Langland implies, through the narratives in which Will is, at last, perhaps in the last times, beginning to participate with real attention. A baptized Christian, he had of course, always heard these narratives but he had also always missed them. Langland's recapitulation of the stories about Christ is markedly resistant to the dominant representations of Christ's humanity in late medieval culture with their expansive, inventively detailed concentration on the tortured, bleeding, honeycombed body as a focus of devotion and imitation.[24] Langland's focus is on the divine power of the Lord Jesus: healer; eschatological prophet who enacts reforms for which the poet and Conscience longed (casting down the stalls of those who turned the "chirche" into a market, XVI.128–129 [Matthew 21:12]); triumphant conqueror of the powers not only through the resurrection but on the cross itself (Jesus, a joy to us all, *jousted* on the cross against death and the devil, destroying their might and making day out of night, XVI.162–166). This power is dazzlingly celebrated in the long account of the Harrowing of Hell as Christ liberates the stolen fruit.[25] In hell, Christ proclaims that he is lord of life, for which he died "today", still thirsting for human souls. With this proclamation he binds Lucifer in chains (XVIII.403[26]). In these foreshadowings of the eschatological consummation, Righteousness and Peace, Truth and Mercy kiss and dance; the *Te Deum* is sung; and the Easter bells are rung for the resurrection. Here it is impossible to separate memory and eschatology, realization and promise as Will calls his wife and daughter to reverence "goddes resurexion", to creep to the cross on knees and kiss it, a saving jewel (XVIII.402–431). In transposing a Good Friday ritual to Easter Sunday, Langland suggests how even in the joyful celebration of the Easter Eucharist, a taste of the fruit for which Will longed, we are penitents living in the shadow and memory of the tree, cross become jewel. In *Piers Plowman* this is a decisive revelation, *de novissimis*, beyond which there will be no going.[27]

Langland's narratives of this revelation do, however, include an unusual inflection that seems essential to his own understanding of eschatological judgment. During the harrowing of hell, Peace (one of the four daughters of God[28]) maintains that when God the Creator became man to save mankind, he committed himself to *learning* something, to *learning* the sorrow of dying (XVIII.212–214). In the Incarnation God risked himself to discover what humanity has suffered, to discover the suffering and pain that overwhelms language. He who knows all joy now learns all woe (XVIII.220–223[29]). Peace fleshes out what Abraham has alluded to earlier when Will encountered him on a mid-Lent Sunday (the fourth Sunday in Lent, when the Epistle is Galatians 4:22–31[30]). There Abraham, the figure of faith, teaches Will that in the Incarnation the creator became creature "to knowe" this state, including the experience of divine abandonment, *"Deus meus, Deus meus, ut quid dereliquisti me?"* (XVI.214–215: Matthew 27:46). In this sharply realized understanding of *kenosis* (Philippians 2:7–8) Langland sees the grounds for his eschatological hope. From the midst of hell, Christ proclaims that his eschatological judgment of humankind will be merciful because he and humans are now brethren of one blood: he will protect his own blood, his kin, reconciled through his grace and purgatory. Here eschatological kindness is rooted in the fact that the king and judge will help his "kynde": "I were an vnkynde kyng but I my kynde helpe" (XVIII.371–403). Through Christ's oration, Langland hints that his understanding of the force and scope of Christ's life, death, and resurrection implies an eschatological kingdom that is far less exclusive than the Augustinian version that had become the Church's.[31] This also confirms an earlier declaration of Christ's when he appeared as the Good Samaritan who saves the abandoned "semyvif [half-alive]" who figures humanity wounded and broken by sin (XVII.51–59). Langland's vision involves a sustained development of traditional exegesis of Luke 10:30–36 and the liturgical filiations of that text.[32] During a long theological dialogue with Will (XVII.83–355), Christ the Samaritan graciously promises that he will be Will's friend and fellow in need (XVII.88–89). Will does not grasp the eschatological reference here, and he does not see that *this* is the very taste of that fruit of the tree of Charity for which he yearned. The offer of friendship is the promise that God in Christ takes full responsibility for "semyvif" in his desperate need. Not that this Samaritan's promise is unconditional. Envisaging reconciliation with God in a thoroughly Trinitarian mode, he warns that one thing can quench the flames of grace that melt the power of the Trinity into merciful forgiveness. That is *unkindness* (XVII.204–320), unkindness against God's creatures (we recall that one of the Creator's names is *Kynde*, for example, XVII.275–276, IX.1–51). Unkindness breaks the bonds of *kinship* with which the Incarnation has identified God. In this sense Langland represents Christ's Incarnation as inaugurating the kingdom into which we either do or do not will to participate now, our will enabled by the gifts left with the innkeeper and inn, Holy Church, the sacraments of Baptism, Penance, and Eucharist (XVII.94–104). The Samaritan *promises* that he will return, for Christ was born to save, with his blood, those who live in faith, hope, and the Church (XVII.112–126). This is the promise of eschatological friendship and kinship.

But this promise has to be received in faith by the community that Christ and the Holy Spirit create. Langland dramatizes this process by having Piers the Plowman (now a figure of St. Peter) build the house or barn of unity ("vnitee, holy chirche on englissh", XIX.182–390). Moving through these foundations, Langland returns to his own era and its Church, a major pre-occupation of the whole poem. But now, because of the work's searchings that have unfolded in convergence with the liturgical representation of salvation history, our perspective has been changed. We are forced to envisage Christian communities under eschatological judgment: "in novissimis temporibus [in the last times]", "in novissimis diebus [in the last days]" (1 Timothy 4:1 and 2 Timothy 3:1), in the time when Christians should discern the presence of antichrists (1 John 2:18). Holy Spirit warns that Antichrist and his disciples will include neo-Constantinian priests, a prophecy already amply fulfilled in *Piers Plowman* (XIX.219–294; see, for example, Prologue 58–79, 83–99; III.35–66; XV.557–561). How does an anti-Joachite poet narrate and dramatize these materials?

Langland has continually insisted that divine forgiveness is conditional on our will to restore the bonds of charity that we have broken, our bonds with others and with God. Being in love and charity with our neighbors, being in "vnite, holy chirche", and participating in the Eucharist has practical consequences: it cannot be only an inward state. As an eschatological community, which is the body of Christ, the Church should enable and embody such acts of mutual forgiveness and restitution, the continual attempt to make a form of life out of following the path of the Samaritan and the "kindness" he has demanded. But at the end of *Piers Plowman* this proves unacceptable to most Christians. They rebel against Conscience's demands that reception of the Eucharist must be preceded by the attempt to fulfill the conditions of the pardon that the risen Christ gave to Piers for dispensation in the Church: *redde quod debes* (XIX.182–198; confirmed by the Holy Spirit, XIX.256–261; see too XI.178–180, 211–212.)[33] The mutiny strives to split apart the sacrament of the altar and the sacrament of penance, a mutiny perhaps replete with harbingers of the future. These Christians are refusing to be a community whose habitual practices incorporate penance, restitution, and forgiveness. They are unwilling to change social practices in any way that would diminish their material profits and habitual forms of exploitation (XIX.391–408, 451–476). They reject the death of the selfhood intrinsic to penance, restitution, and forgiveness. They thus reject habits on which a Eucharistic and eschatological community, according to Langland, must be built. We seem to be on very familiar ground (Prologue, I. 1–9, VI–VII, X.13–136, XV). But readers now know that we and all such ordinary, daily, naturalized acts of rebellion stand under eschatological judgment, "in novissimis temporibus". Seeing in this light, may make us see differently. Furthermore, the fact of being "in novissimis temporibus" is brought home to the body of Will. The figure of the poet depicts his own body being crushed by old age: with death approaching, "for drede gan I quake" (XX.183–200). In his need he receives divine counsel that he should commit himself to the house of unity, Holy Church: this is the eschatological barn in which he should continue the task of learning to love until God sends for him (XX.212–216).

But the Church into which Will has been ordered to remain is now subjected to the remorselessly critical account that has pervaded *Piers Plowman*, one that has gone far beyond the horizons of traditional satire.[34] Once more we are shown the late medieval Church as being thoroughly immersed in pursuits of the market, in simony and in the desire for worldly power (XX.121–128, 217–229). But now these practices are understood as the effects of Antichrist's presence *within* the Church (XX.52–64, 128). For Langland, this presence seems especially clear in the transformation of the sacrament of penance into a commodity and in the role of modern friars (XX.280–379[35]). This does not seem very much like the Church of Augustine, or John Milbank for that matter, Christ's kingdom on earth.[36] For Langland, the Church has become an eschatological community that is acting in many ways as an impediment to its members' recognition of their eschatological salvation. Word and sacrament become forces of *amnesia* luring us into easy conformity with a culture that, according to Langland, draws its subjects into worship of the world (I.1–9, but *passim*). Word and sacrament now stifle the sources of contrition and conversion (XX.356–372). Contrition is drugged and enchanted in the confessional so that Christians cease even to fear sin (XX.373–379; XX.53–61, 64). Only, it seems, a few "fools" resist Antichrist within the Church (XX.61, 74–77). In the last seven lines of the poem, Conscience, made constable of Holy Church by the Holy Spirit (XX.314–315) determines to leave the Church, in search of Piers the Plowman and a solution to the symptomatic problem of the friars. With this, he sets out after Grace (XX.380–386).

What are we to make of this ending?[37] For the Holy Spirit's constable to be forced out of the Church in search of Piers ("*Petrus id est Christus*", St. Peter, one who figures the eschatological fulfillment of humanity) seems a catastrophic reflection on the contemporary Church. Can such a community, one where sacraments are used as drugs of enchantment, be the ark outside of which *nulla salus*? Against many appearances, Langland's answer is a carefully qualified "yes". The answer "no" would have taken him down the path followed by his contemporary John Wyclif, a path leading to the denial that there is any identity between the Roman Church and the Church of the creed.[38] But how can the affirmative answer be maintained in the face of such a devastating representation of the Church? The answer unfolds from Kind's order that Will should live the remainder of his life in the Church, learning to love, an order that is unconditional (XX.201–206). Will obeys, as we noted, without reservation. He stays in the Church despite its infiltration by the forces of Antichrist. With him too are those committed to resisting these forces, resisters currently judged to be "fools" (XX.61, 74–77: using 1 Corinthians 1:20–31). So while Will, the figure of the poet stays, the divinely appointed constable leaves in search of an apparently absent Piers and Grace. That the Church's Conscience is driven to this move gives no encouragement, let alone license, to any individual Christian or group of Christians to "leave" the Church despite its apparent collapse in the face of Antichrist's invasions. Nor, in Langland's ending, is there the remotest sanction for any neo-Joachite expectations of a new *status* of bliss within history. Readers will *remember* that Christ the Samaritan personally placed "semyvif" within the inn, which is the Church, giving all the necessary resources and livelihood until his return (XVII.66–82). Will and his readers are in the position of "semyvif", kept alive by the Samaritan's gifts bestowed on the inn. We have no licence to think that we ourselves can carry these essential resources off to another inn of our imagination, or purchase substitutes in the market, or survive without them. True enough, the Samaritan gave no indication that the inn would be invaded by the forces of Antichrist, by drugs and enchantments in the ways so graphically evoked by the poet. Nevertheless, Holy Spirit, in the apostolic Church, had warned that such would be our plight (XIX.215–226). However confusing and painful this is, however wrathful the poet's representations of his Church, he never suggests that abandoning the visible inn is an option for Christians. We are compelled to acknowledge that this ambivalent, invaded place *is* the divinely given eschatological community, and *this* is what living in such a community in the last times actually means. Members are lured by opiates and enchantments passed off as divine medicines, menaced by illusion and terror. Nor can we have any clear idea of the hour (Acts 1:7, Matthew 24:36) although we know that death presses towards us. The Samaritan's gracious friendship and his promise to help us in time of need (XVII.88–89; XVIII.365–431) are now memories. Their present and future realities remain hidden. Despite the gifts of Christ and the Holy Spirit poured into the Church, gifts that include *Piers Plowman*, the Church is not, emphatically not, the kingdom of God. It stands, with its members, under judgment for its *amnesia*, its substitutions of enchanting drugs for divine gifts, its endless collusions with organized violence (slavery, cruel exploitation, war, torture), its collusion with powerful forces it fails to recognize as Antichrist's. Now, at the end of the poem, we have to recognize such failings as eschatological ones. The poem's representations of the Church are certainly antithetical to any triumphalist narratives of the Church, medieval or contemporary. But then Langland would encourage us to see such triumphal models as among the opiates available in the Church, ones inducing an enchanting *amnesia*. Faith, "in novissimis temporibus" is enacted by Will: obediently he remains in the Church, invaded as it is by Antichrist, apparently abandoned even by its constable, Conscience. His patience is trust in the promises Christ has given, as Samaritan, as liberator of souls in the prisons of hell and as resurrected Son of God.

NOTES

1 Rowan Williams, *Resurrection: Interpreting the Easter Gospel* (Harrisburg, PA: Morehouse, 1994), p. 63.
2 The critical editions of these versions of *Piers Plowman* are the following: *Piers Plowman: The A Version*, ed. G. Kane (London: Athlone Press, 1960); *Piers Plowman: The B Version*, ed. G. Kane and E. Talbot Donaldson (London: Athlone Press, 1975, rev. 1988); *Piers Plowman: The C Version*, ed. G. Russell and G. Kane (London: Athlone Press, 1997). Some consider the composite version in the Bodleian Library, MS Bodley 851, ff 124–208, to be a fourth version; it was edited by A. G. Rigg and C. Brewer as *Piers Plowman: The Z Version* (Toronto: Pontifical Institute, 1983). On the latter, however, see Ralph Hanna, "Studies in the MSS of *Piers Plowman*", *Yearbook of Langland Studies* 7 (1993), pp. 1–25 and Kane, "The 'Z Version' of *Piers Plowman*", *Speculum* 60 (1985), pp. 910–930. In the present essay I work from Kane and Donaldson's edition of the B version. There is an excellent translation of this version

by Donaldson, an ideal place from which to begin teaching the work: *Piers Plowman*, ed. Elizabeth D. Kirk and Judith H. Anderson (London: Norton, 1990); there is also a good translation of the C version by George Economou, *Piers Plowman* (Philadelphia, PA: University of Pennsylvania Press, 1996).

3 Wyclif describes this office as the most worldly in the kingdom in *De Blasphemia*, ed. M. H. Dziewicki (London: Wyclif Society, 1893), p. 194. I am obviously summarizing a complex and hardly transparent history. The best introduction remains Rodney Hilton, *Bond Men Made Free* (London: Temple Smith, 1973), with R. W. Kaeuper, *War, Justice, and Public Order: England and France in the Later Middle Ages* (Oxford: Clarendon Press, 1988), chapter 4.

4 Here too I summarize a complex history with a substantial literature. The following offer the most helpful introduction: Peter Heath, *Church and Realm, 1272–1461* (London: Fontana, 1988); Peter McNiven, *Heresy and Politics in the Reign of Henry IV* (Woodbridge, UK: Boydell Press, 1987); Margaret Aston, "Lollardy and Sedition, 1381–1431", *Past and Present* 17 (1960), pp. 1–44; Paul Strohm, *England's Empty Throne* (New Haven, CT: Yale University Press, 1998), chapters 2 and 5. On Wyclif and Wycliffism, see Anne Hudson, *The Premature Reformation* (Oxford: Clarendon Press, 1988) and Aston, *Faith and Fire* (London: Hambledon Press, 1993), chapters 1–4, 8–10. For Wyclif's views on the 1383 crusade into Flanders, led by Bishop Despenser, Julian of Norwich's bishop, see *De Solucione Sathane* (chapter 2) in *Polemical Works in Latin*, ed. R. Buddensieg (London: Wyclif Society, 1883), 2:296; on Wyclif's eschatology, see Penn Szittya, *The Antifraternal Tradition in Medieval Literature* (Princeton, NJ: Princeton University Press, 1986), chapter 4.

5 For the most sustained attempts to Joachize *Piers Plowman*, see M. W. Bloomfield, *Piers Plowman as a Fourteenth Century Apocalypse* (New Brunswick, NJ: Rutgers University Press, 1961), chapters 4–5; Bloomfield, "*Piers Plowman* and the three grades of charity", *Anglia* 76 (1958), pp. 227–253; Kathryn Kerby-Fulton, *Reformist Apocalypticism and Piers Plowman* (Cambridge: Cambridge University Press, 1990), *passim* but especially chapter 5. For criticism of such Joachizing see Robert Adams, "Some versions of apocalypse: learned and popular eschatology in *Piers Plowman*", in *The Popular Literature of Medieval England*, ed. Thomas J. Heffernan (Knoxville, TN: University of Tennessee Press, 1985), pp. 194–236; Richard Emmerson, " 'Yernen to rede redeles?' *Piers Plowman* and Prophecy", *Yearbook of Langland Studies* 7 (1993), pp. 28–76, see esp. pp. 32–38, pp. 41–49; Emmerson, *Antichrist in the Middle Ages* (Seattle, WA: University of Washington Press, 1981), pp. 193–203; Willi Erzgraeber, "Apokalypse und Antichrist in der englischer Literatur des 14. Jahrhunderts: William Langlands *Piers Plowman*, Joachim von Fiore und der Chiliasmus des Mittelalters", *Literaturwissenschaftliches Jahrbuch im Auftrage der Gorres Gesellschaft* 29 (1988), pp. 233–252.

6 There is now a substantial and responsible literature on Joachim and Joachism. From this I have found the following especially helpful: Marjorie Reeves and Beatrice Hirsch-Reich, *The Figurae of Joachim of Fiore* (Oxford: Clarendon Press, 1972); Reeves, *The Influence of Prophecy in the Later Middle Ages* (Oxford: Oxford University Press, 1969); Bernard McGinn, *Visions of the End* (New York, NY: Columbia University Press, 1979), pp. 126–141, pp. 196–202, pp. 203–221; Gordon Leff, *Heresy in the Later Middle Ages*, 2 vols. (Manchester: Manchester University Press, 1967), vol 1: part 1; David Burr, *Olivi's Peaceable Kingdom: A Reading of the Apocalyptic Commentary* (Philadelphia, PA: University of Pennsylvania Press, 1993). Finally, from my own concerns, most important of all is Henri de Lubac, *Exégèse Médiévale*, 2 parts in 4 vols. (Paris: Aubier, 1959–1964), II.1, chapter 6 and II.2, chapter 9, sections 4–5.

7 See especially St. Augustine, *The City of God*, trans. H. Bettenson (London: Penguin, 1984), XVIII.51–53; on Augustine here, see Paula Fredriksen, "Apocalypse and Redemption: From John of Patmos to Augustine of Hippo", *Vigiliae Christianae* 45 (1991), pp. 151–183. For de Lubac's demonstration of Joachim's rupture with these exegetical traditions, see references at the end of n. 5.

8 See Bernard McGinn, *The Calabrian Abbot, Joachim of Fiore in the History of Western Thought* (New York, NY: Macmillan, 1985), chapter 6, especially pp. 190–192 and p. 202 n. 194; de Lubac *Exégèse Médiévale*, II.1, pp. 454–455, pp. 461–464, pp. 473–475, pp. 481–482, pp. 501–527, p. 546; Leff, *Heresy*, I.72–76, part one *passim*. On Gerardo of Borgo San Donnino's *Introductorium in Evangelium Eternum*, see Burr, *Peaceable Kingdom*, pp. 9–10, pp. 14–19 with de Lubac, *Exégèse Médiévale*, II.1, pp. 401–463.

9 Jean de Roquetaillade provides striking examples of such developments: see Jeanne Bignami-Odier, *Études sur Jean de Roquetaillade (Johannes de Rupescissa)*, (Paris: Vrin, 1952),

p. 85, p. 94, pp. 102–104, pp. 123–125, pp. 157–173; also, Reeves, *Influence,* pp. 225–227, pp. 321–324.

10   In *Opera Omnia,* vol. 15 (25 vols., New York, NY: Musurgia, 1948–50), pp. 1–75: here see chapter 23, pp. 69–71.

11   *Summa Theologiae,* Latin and English translation, Blackfriars edition, vol. 30 (London: Eyre and Spottiswoode, 1972), I–II.106–114; here, I–II.106.4; quotations, *seriatim,* from 106.4, *resp; ad 2; ad 4.* On Thomas's critique of Joachim, see McGinn, *Calabrian Abbot,* pp. 211–212 and "The Abbot and the Doctors", *Church History* 40 (1971), pp. 30–47.

12   For these representations see the poem's Prologue; Langland's critical engagement with his polity is pursued with great energy from passus I–VI, and X.13–119 and XIII–XIV. While the representations of the Church are woven in here, his most concentrated critique is offered in XV and XX. I give references to passus and line (from the Kane and Donaldson B version, see n. 2) in the text.

13   In this brief essay I cannot even summarize these; for an introduction see *A Companion to Piers Plowman,* ed. John A. Alford (Berkeley, CA: University of California Press, 1988); James Simpson, *Piers Plowman: An Introduction to the B-text* (London: Longman, 1990); David Aers, *Community, Gender, and Individual Identity, English Writing, 1360–1430* (London: Routledge, 1988), chapter 1; Anne Middleton, "William Langland's 'Kynde Name': Authorial Signature and Social Identity in Late Fourteenth-Century England", in *Literary Practice and Social Change in Britain, 1380–1530,* ed. Lee Patterson (Berkeley, CA: University of California Press, 1990), pp. 15–82.

14   See V.510–VII.206; see Matthew 5–6 and Luke 6:20–38 alongside passus VII.122–135. On the Statute of Laborers (1351) and Piers's conversion, see Aers, *Community,* chapter 1; on the 1388 Statute and the later version of *Piers Plowman,* see Anne Middleton, "Acts of Vagrancy: The C Version 'Autobiography' and the Statute of 1388", in *Written Work,* ed. Steven Justice and Kathryn Kerby-Fulton (Philadelphia, PA: University of Pennsylvania Press, 1997), pp. 208–317.

15   J. A. W. Bennett, ed., *Piers Plowman: The Prologue and Passus I–VII* (Oxford: Clarendon Press, 1972), p. 141; for the conversion of the Jews as a marker of the end of history, see St. Augustine, *City of God,* XX.29. Conscience's riddle is in a conventional apocalyptic and prophetic mode.

16   A related passage is X.332–335. See the works cited in n. 5, especially works by Adams and Erzgraeber, contrasting with the Joachizing readings of Bloomfield, *Piers Plowman,* pp. 112–114 and Kerby-Fulton, *Reformist Apocalypticism,* pp. 180–200.

17   Bignami-Odier, *Études sur Jean de Roquetaillade,* p. 94, pp. 102–104, pp. 123–124, pp. 170–172. For an unwarranted attempt to read "oon cristene kyng" as Christ, see Adams, "Some versions", pp. 211–213.

18   de Lubac, *Exégèse Médiévale,* II.1, p. 538; for a careful account of the evidence for this judgment, II.1, chapter 6; also McGinn, *Calabrian Abbot,* pp. 125–127, pp. 137–138, where the sympathetic author concedes that the humanity of Christ, and its centrality in traditional exegesis, is displaced. For other passages explicitly dealing with apocalyptic modes and millenarian perspectives, see Prologue, 64–67, VI.321–331, X.322–335, XV.546–567.

19   For St. Thomas on Conscience, *ST,* I–II.19.5–6; on conscience in medieval thought, see Timothy C. Potts, *Conscience in Medieval Philosophy* (Cambridge: Cambridge University Press, 1980) and chapter 36 in *The Cambridge History of Later Medieval Philosophy,* ed. Norman Kretzmann *et al.* (Cambridge: Cambridge University Press, 1982). See too M. C. Schroeder [Carruthers], "The Character of Conscience in *Piers Plowman*", *Studies in Philology* 67 (1970), pp. 13–30.

20   On the allegory and history here, see David Aers, *Piers Plowman and Christian Allegory* (London: Arnold, 1975), pp. 90–109.

21   I wrote against this habit in *Piers Plowman,* pp. 101–105, but that seems to have had no effect on subsequent readings of the poem.

22   Quotations from the Bible are from the Douai-Rheims translation of the Vulgate, the medieval Bible: *The Holy Bible* (London: Burns and Oates, 1964). On medieval readings and rewritings of the Song of Songs, see E. Ann Matter, *The Voice of My Beloved: The Song of Songs in Western Medieval Christianity* (Philadelphia, PA: Pennsylvania University Press, 1990); Ann W. Astell, *The Song of Songs in the Middle Ages* (Ithaca, NY: Cornell University Press, 1990); W. Riehle, *The Middle English Mystics* (London: Routledge, 1981), chapter 3.

23   Bernard of Clairvaux, *On the Song of Songs*, trans. K. Walsh and I. M. Edmonds, vol. 3
      (Kalamazoo, MI: Cistercian Publications, 1979), see sermons 48–51, pp. 11–48; quotation
      here is from 48.3.6 (p. 17) glossed through 48.3.7 (pp. 18–19). One could also consider
      Nicholas of Lyra's most unBernardine reading of the Songs: he takes the fruit of 7:8 as
      representing the sweetness experienced in the heights of contemplation, the apple tree of
      8:5 as Christ, and warns against mistaking "malo" in "sub arbore malo" (8:5) for the fruit
      of the forbidden tree; see *The Postilla of Nicholas of Lyra on the Song of Songs*, trans. and ed.
      J. G. Kiecker (Milwaukee, WI: Marquette University Press, 1998), p. 106, pp. 112–114. It
      should be noted that Kiecker's introduction on Nicholas of Lyra as exegete is strangely
      inadequate; compare de Lubac *Exégèse Médiévale*, II.2, pp. 344–358 and Burr, *Peaceable
      Kingdom*, pp. 251–254.

24   For exemplification, reference to the secondary literature, and analysis, see David Aers
      and Lynn Staley, *Powers of the Holy: Religion, Politics, and Gender in Late Medieval English
      Culture* (University Park, PA: Pennsylvania State University Press, 1996), chapters 1–2. For
      a contrasting approach, see Ellen M. Ross, *The Grief of God* (New York, NY: Oxford
      University Press, 1997).

25   On the harrowing of hell in *Piers Plowman*, see C. W. Marx, *The Devil's Rights and Redemption*
      (Cambridge: Brewer, 1995), pp. 103–113; for its treatment in a Joachizing study, Bloomfield,
      Piers Plowman, pp. 123–125.

26   See St. Augustine, *City of God*, XX.7, on this binding and Apocalypse 20; here Christ fulfills
      his promise in passus XVII.111–114; on this, see Adams, "Some Versions", p. 203.

27   For Langland, as for St. Thomas, this revelation "does not belong only to Christ but also to
      the Holy Spirit", *ST* I–II.106–4 *ad* 3; see *Piers Plowman*, XVI.18–66, 86–94, 176–272; XVII.
      127–356; XIX.182–273.

28   See Hope Traver, *The Four Daughters of God* (Philadelphia, PA: Bryn Mawr Monographs,
      1907) and "The Four Daughters of God: a mirror of changing doctrine", *PMLA* 40 (1925),
      pp. 44–92.

29   Aers, *Piers Plowman*, pp. 106–109.

30   On Langland's use of the liturgy here, see M. F. Vaughan, "The Liturgical Perspectives of
      Piers Plowman, B, XVI–XIX", *Studies in Medieval and Renaissance History* 3 (1980), pp. 87–155.

31   See G. H. Russell, "The Salvation of the Heathen: The Exploration of a Theme in *Piers
      Plowman*", *Journal of the Warburg and Courtauld Institute* 29 (1966), pp. 101–116 and Nicholas
      Watson, "Visions of Inclusion: Universal Salvation and Vernacular Theology in Pre-
      Reformation England", *Journal of Medieval and Early Modern Studies* 27 (1997), pp. 145–187,
      esp. pp. 153–166.

32   The parable of the good Samaritan is read on the thirteenth Sunday after Trinity. For the
      exegetical tradition, see Ben Smith, *Traditional Imagery of Charity in Piers Plowman* (The Hague:
      Mouton, 1966), chapter 4; for the liturgy here, Vaughan, "The Liturgical Perspectives",
      pp. 117–123 and R. St.-Jacques, "The Liturgical Association of Langland's Samaritan",
      Traditio 25 (1969), pp. 217–230.

33   On *redde quod debes*, see R. W. Frank, *Piers Plowman and the Scheme of Salvation* (New Haven,
      CT: Yale University Press, 1957), 106–109; Bloomfield, *Piers Plowman*, 130–134; Britton J.
      Harwood, *Piers Plowman and the Problem of Belief* (Toronto: University of Toronto Press,
      1992), 114–116, 125–126, 130–132, 137.

34   See David Aers, *Chaucer, Langland, and the Creative Imagination* (London: Routledge and
      Kegan Paul, 1980), chapter 2; Wendy Scase, *Piers Plowman and the New Anticlericalism*
      (Cambridge: Cambridge University Press, 1989).

35   On Langland and the friars, Szittya, *The Antifraternal Tradition*, chapter 7.

36   For St. Augustine, *City of God*, XVII.4; for example, "Dicat ergo ecclesia Christi, civitas regis
      magni, gratia plena, prole fecunda [Therefore, let the Church of Christ speak, the city of the
      great king, full of grace, fruitful in children", *De Civitate Dei*, ed. B. Dombart and A. Kalb
      (5th ed., Stuttgart: Teubner, 1993), 2:205; the translation is slightly altered from Bettenson's
      (n. 7); also XIX.17, in which the Church is seen as the heavenly city on pilgrimage; and XX.9,
      where the Church is called the kingdom of Christ and kingdom of heaven ("ecclesia
      regnum eius regnumve caelorum", 2:428; also, "ecclesia regnum Christi est regnumque
      caelorum", 2:429; and "ad ecclesiam, quod est regnum Christi", 2:431). For John Milbank,
      see *Theology and Social Theory* (Oxford: Blackwell, 1990), pp. 402–408, where St. Augustine
      is hailed as propagating the vision of the Church congenial to Milbank, for whom the

Church is "the city of God" (p. 405; see too p. 403). Reluctantly, so it seems to me, Milbank concedes that St. Augustine's espousal of secular forms of coercion does introduce "an ambiguity", but his rather platonizing approach to the Church's history delivers him from getting specific and encourages a move to "ontology" (pp. 419–432).

37   For a representational range of answers to this question: Aers, *Chaucer, Langland,* pp. 59–61, pp. 76–79; Emmerson, *Antichrist,* pp. 200–202; Bloomfield, *Piers Plowman,* pp. 147–149, p. 153; Szittya, *Antifraternal Tradition,* pp. 247–287; Simpson, *Piers Plowman,* pp. 234–245.

38   For a good introduction to Wycliffite ecclesiology, see Anne Hudson, *The Premature Reformation,* chapter 7.

CHAPTER 2

NIRVANA AS THE LAST THING?
THE ICONIC END OF THE
NARRATIVE IMAGINATION[1]

PAUL J. GRIFFITHS

In this essay I argue that the life of the world to come, the hoped-for final end of the individual Christian (and perhaps of all people), cannot be characterized or represented narratively because attempts so to represent it are always both incoherent and idolatrous; that the life of the world to come can be represented both formally and iconically; and that what Buddhists have said about Nirvana may serve Christians in the development of more adequate formal and iconic representations of the life of the world to come. This is, then, an essay in Christian theology understood principally as an abstract elucidation of some syntactical elements in the Christian master text, and secondarily as commentary upon some semantic elements therein.

The essay is undertaken with an eye to some resources in Buddhist thought (though these resources won't be treated explicitly until close to its end). Since Christian theology is an omnivorous beast (which is another way of saying that it is catholic), little apology is needed, I think, for making use of such resources. Anything of use to the Church's enterprise of coming to understand more fully the message with the preservation and transmission of which it is charged ought to be used; and there is no good theological reason for thinking that useful materials are to be found only among those things that Christians have thought and said. But it is important to note that "Buddhism" in this essay is used very much as "Christianity" is: as synecdoche for "Buddhist master text", which in turn is (my understanding of) a collection of semantic items and syntactical rules for combination of those items at a much higher level of abstraction than anything found in any actual Buddhist literary works or practices. I shall only occasionally descend

Paul J. Griffiths
The Divinity School, University of Chicago, Chicago, IL 60637, USA

to the level of such particulars. This is not because I have any objection to considering them. Indeed, it seems to me that the deep nourishment of Christian theology by religiously alien traditions such as Buddhism will only be achieved by serious attention to just such specifics, an attention that requires a kind of deep, serious, and concentrated reading whose archetypal literary product is the commentary. But this essay is not an appropriate vehicle for that enterprise; it must remain at a much more abstract level.

Eschatology: Some Distinctions

Eschatology's topic is the *eschata*, the last things, and its content is the thoughts and words produced by considering this topic. It has two domains: the individual and the universal. Individual eschatology interests itself in the last things of particular objects or states of affairs. It is interested in, for instance, the end of this man, that horse, the book on the shelf over there, the Tudor dynasty, the Clinton presidency. Universal eschatology, by contrast, is interested in the last things of the universe considered as a whole.

Both individual and universal eschatology are concerned with endings of temporal sequences. If there are last things there must have been preceding things (even if not first things), even if the temporal gap separating them is vanishingly small: the feeble apocalypse of a clock's tock can be what it is (an ending, a last thing) only because there was the humble genesis of its tick (a beginning, a first thing).[2] But endings, whether of individuals or of the universe, are not all of one conceptual kind, and eschatology must be further analyzed according to different senses of "ending". Three such senses will be important for this essay.

First, there are endings understood as terminations. A termination is the simple ending of an unnarratable temporal sequence, which is to say the bringing to a halt of a sequence without *telos*, without aim or goal, and therefore also without possibility of closure. It is precisely because of the absence of *telos* that such sequences cannot be represented by a narrative, though they may be represented in other ways. Consider the *Annals of St. Gall*, in which the entry for the year A.D. 709 reads "Hard winter. Duke Gottfried died", and that for 710 reads "Hard year and deficient in crops".[3] An annal lists a sequence of events like these without turning them into a narrative, which is to say (partially, but most importantly) without turning the events into a plot—without, as the narratologists would say, emplotting them. A plot (without which there is no narrative) requires a goal, an end, the possibility of completion: it demands that the sequence of events it treats be presented as (and be capable of being seen as) directed and meaningful. A sequence treated by an annalist is, by contrast, presented as a list, as one damn thing after another, without expectation or possibility of resolution or closure. The presentation of such a sequence must either terminate or extend infinitely; its ideal type, perhaps, would be a description of someone announcing, one after another, each numeral in the series of natural numbers. Temporal sequences incapable of emplotment need not only be represented annalistically; they can also be represented formally or iconically (and perhaps in other ways too). I'll say more about these possibilities below.

Second, there are endings understood as truncations. A truncation is the unexpected and inappropriate ending of a narratable temporal sequence, an ending by which the goal or aim of the sequence is cut off, its proper development curtailed. A sequence of this sort does possess a *telos*, and may be represented narratively, with emplotment and the other devices that jointly constitute a narrative. But its goal is not realized; the sequence (and any narrative representing it) ends prematurely. A literary presentation of a narratable (and narrated) sequence is not often truncated, for obvious reasons; this usually occurs when, as with Dickens's *Edwin Drood*, authors are unable to bring a narrative to an end for reasons beyond their control. A decision as to whether truncation is common in life, rather than literature, must rest upon more fundamental metaphysical convictions; but there are certainly many endings which most of us would think of as truncations. The chrysalis is crushed underfoot before it can become a butterfly; the organism dies by violence before transmitting its DNA; the performance of *Die Zauberflöte* is brought to a halt by the sudden heart attack of the man singing Papageno in the first act (perhaps as he launches into the "Schnelle Füße, rascher Mut", with Pamina). All these events seem to prevent the sequence of which they form a part from reaching its implied goal or end, and in so doing to truncate it.

Third, there are endings understood as completions. A completion is the full and final ending of a narratable temporal sequence, an ending by which the goal or aim of the sequence is realized, and (when presented literarily) made evident. Temporal sequences ended by completion are in every respect like those ended by truncation, except that they are not prematurely cut off. Their literary presentation will be more like *Great Expectations* than *Edwin Drood*; and in life they may be typified by the chrysalis becoming a butterfly.

Eschatology, whether individual or universal, may be concerned with endings (last things) in any or all of these senses. A particular thing might be thought of and represented as ending by termination, truncation, or completion; so might the universe. But a final distinction (in the shape of a warning) is useful at this point. It is the distinction between transitional and final eschatology. The former treats the events immediately preceding, leading up to, and culminating in the final event, the end (whether termination, truncation, or completion); but it does not treat what follows that final event, for that is the topic of final eschatology. Suppose the temporal sequence treated is the aforementioned truncated performance of *Die Zauberflöte*. Its last thing, we might say, is the ringing down of the curtain upon a scene of chaos shortly after the collapse of Papageno. Transitional eschatology would treat the signs of this end: the wavering and physical uncertainty of Papageno in the moments before the collapse, the reactions of the rest of the cast and the audience to these symptoms, and so on. But transitional eschatology would stop with the curtain's descent, for that would decisively mark the end of the performance. Final eschatology would pick up at this point, and would ask what can be said about the performance after its end. The answer to the final-eschatological question in the case of sequences that end by truncation or termination will usually (though not always, as will become clear) be "nothing". That particular performance is simply over; it has no future of which to speak, just as there is nothing to be said about the recitation of an infinite series of numbers after its termination (other than that it has been terminated).

Transitional eschatology, then, treats the events leading up to and culminating in the end of a sequence; final eschatology treats what is to be said about that sequence upon its ending. Transitional eschatology is only eschatology by courtesy, as it were; it bears much the same relation to final eschatology (which is eschatology proper) as obstetrics does to pediatrics. The warning connected with the distinction between transitional and final eschatology is, then, not to treat the former as though it were the latter: it is the latter (final eschatology) that raises the interesting theoretical and theological questions, and it is exclusively the latter with which this essay will be concerned.

These distinctions yield the following picture. Final eschatology is of two kinds according to whether it treats the ends of particular things and states of affairs (individual eschatology), or the end of everything (universal eschatology). Each of these has three further kinds, depending upon how the ends in question are construed, yielding: individual final eschatology concerned with terminations, truncations, or completions; and universal final eschatology concerned with the same three ends.

Individual final eschatology understood in this way is of interest to most human beings. Almost everyone considers what to think and say about their own end, and in doing so engages in one or more of the kinds of eschatology mentioned. And, of course, eschatology in theoretic or dramatic dress is found almost everywhere: there are Marxist, Buddhist, Islamic, and even democratic eschatologies, as well as literary ones without clear and obvious affiliation to any religion or political ideology. As a result, while the term "eschatology" is a technical one that belongs to Christian theology, that to which it refers is by no means so limited. This essay, while it is an exercise in Christian theology, will be concerned to do what it does in that sphere in explicit awareness of and interaction with at least one other species of eschatology: that belonging to Indian Buddhist thought and centering around the idea of Nirvana. But before proceeding to the constructive parts of this essay it is important to say a little more (in regrettably abstract and didactic fashion) about the semantics and syntax of specifically Christian eschatology.

Christian Eschatology

Christian theologians (and many Christians who are not theologians) have been interested in most (though not all) of the kinds of eschatology already mentioned. A large proportion of what is usually called eschatology by theologians and historians of Christianity, though, is what I have called transitional eschatology: it is literary or conceptual material that treats the events leading up to the end, events that mark the transition from what can be narrated to what cannot. The story (whether of an individual or of the universe) approaches its completion (or truncation) by way of events that can be narrated because they are (still) capable of emplotment. Most apocalyptic literature, including most of the Book of Revelation and the other biblical apocalypses, represents transitional rather than final eschatology, and this is a large part of its attraction. There is still a story to tell, and often a dramatic and highly-colored one. When we read of the Son of Man coming with the clouds of heaven, trailing glory (Dan. 7:14), or of the Lamb opening the seven-sealed book (Rev. 6), or of the sun darkening and the stars falling from heaven (Mark 13:24–25), or of the Day of the Lord (Isa. 26–29), we are reading transitional eschatology, not final eschatology.[4] Many traditional Christian concepts, for example that of purgatory, also move in the sphere of transitional rather than final eschatology, for here too there is still a story to tell, the story of purification from sin before entry upon final beatitude. I shall not be further concerned with this material in what follows.

Christian theology also treats final eschatology in both its universal and individual kinds. In neither case does it envisage the possibility of endings understood as terminations. This is because it is intrinsic to Christian thought to understand the sequence of events that constitutes the history of the universe, as well as the sequence that constitutes the history of each individual within it, as narratable, which is to say as bearing the weight of a goal or purpose. Any such sequence must end either by truncation (when its purpose is not realized), or by completion (when it is). Termination is an ending possible only for unnarratable sequences, and as a result the last things of the universe and of every individual within it cannot, from the viewpoint of Christian theology, be seen as a termination; they can be seen only as a truncation or a completion.

Christians are committed to seeing both the events of their own lives and those of the universe as narratable because that is how the Bible presents them and that is how the Church has consistently interpreted and represented what the Bible says. The universe has a narratable beginning: *bereshith*, "in the beginning" (Gen. 1:1);[5] it has a narrative crux, which is the birth, death, and resurrection of Jesus of Nazareth; and it will have an end in which the fabric of the heavens will be rolled up like a scroll (Rev. 6:14), and with which the Lord Jesus's coming again will be inextricably associated (Rev. 22:20). The ending is implied already in the beginning: the *explicit* was implicit in the *incipit*, and each moment between is a *kairos*, a God-given opportune moment. The life of each individual, too, is narratable, and in a similar way: it begins in the womb, finds its crux in Jesus of Nazareth (Rom. 6:4–11), and looks forward in hope to a final resurrection of the body (1 Cor. 15). The narratability of the universe's history and of the history of each individual within it is a central syntactical principle of Christian thought. This principle implies a final eschatology with respect to both kinds of history, and one that can be construed only in terms of truncation or completion.

A further general point can be made about the syntax of Christian eschatology. It is that there is an important dissimilarity between what Christians must say in final-eschatological voice about the universe, and what we must say about individuals within it. The universe's final end must be understood as a completion rather than a truncation, while each individual may end either by truncation or by completion. Why the difference? The universe's completion is guaranteed by the axiom that God's purposes for the whole cannot be frustrated; this means that the *telos* (whatever exactly it is) of the universe must be realized, which is also to say that its final end must be a completion, rather than a truncation (or a termination). To deny that this is so would be to deny that the labor pains of the created order (Rom. 8:22) will issue in birth; it would also be to deny the universal transformative efficacy of the cross and the resurrection, and so to deny the necessity and effect of the incarnation, as well as the essentially triune nature of God. The universe's final end, then, cannot but be a completion, and it is a central function of Christian final eschatology to indicate this fact. For Christians, one of the functions of the theological virtue of faith is precisely to provide knowledge that the necessary and inevitable final end of the universe will be a completion (though not to provide knowledge of the exact nature of this completion).

But it is different with the last things of individuals. According to Christian theology, these may be either truncations or completions, which is to say that each individual may be either damned or saved. When the narratable sequence of the events of the life of an individual does not issue in a realization of the *telos* of that individual's life, there is truncation. And when the sequence does issue in such a realization, there is completion. Truncation is possible, of course, because each individual may refuse the gift of salvation offered by God. No matter how often and how violently the three-person'd God batters the heart with that gift, it can be refused. And when the gift is systematically and consistently refused, the *telos* of the refuser's life cannot be realized precisely because that *telos* is to be understood formally as repeated acceptance of God's gift. Christians must allow the possibility of individual final ends that are truncations on pain of denying human freedom, just as we must allow the possibility of individual final ends that are completions on pain of denying God's power and love.

Another asymmetry should now be evident: it is syntactically impossible for Christian final eschatology to affirm the possibility that all individual final ends might be truncations (that damnation might be universal); but the affirmation that all individual final ends might be completions (that salvation might be universal) is syntactically required.[6] Notice, too, that the positions described in this and the preceding paragraph say nothing about the possibility of knowing whether any particular individual will meet a final end that is a truncation or one that is a completion. Such knowledge is certainly impossible for us with respect to anyone now living; it is largely impossible, too, with respect to anyone who has died.[7] The relevant theological virtue here is hope: by it, we Christians hope for our own salvation (for the completion of our narrative rather than its truncation), for the salvation of those we love, and for the salvation of all. But none of these things can be known in our epistemically limited condition here below.

The upshot of these remarks is that Christian theology concerns itself with both individual and universal final eschatology; that it places the latter under the rubric of completion and the former under the rubrics of both truncation and completion; and that it thereby rules out the possibility of simple termination for both individuals and the universe.

This sketch of the syntax of Christian eschatology permits a precise framing of the central question of this essay: How may Christians represent the last things of individuals, their final ends? What discursive possibilities are there for the representation of truncation or completion so far as individuals are concerned?

Completion and After

It follows from the definitions so far given that the sequence of events by which an individual's life is made up can no longer be narrated after completion has been reached. Completion entails the impossibility of further narrative representation because such representation requires emplotment, which in turn requires a teleological order, a sequence of events aimed at closure. But with completion, closure has been attained and the *telos* has been reached. No further emplotment is possible: there is no narrator, no narratee, no subject, no dramatic tension, no resolution, no progress. This begins to sound like simple cessation: the end of the individual whose life has reached its completion. But any such view is ruled out by the syntax of Christian faith and hope, as already indicated: completion, for Christians, entails not an ending or an emptiness, but a radical remaking that is a fulfilment as well as a kind of beginning,[8] the *resurrectio mortuorum et vita venturi saeculi*. But how then, if not narratively, is this life of the world to come to be represented?

Christians have certainly thought it important to represent it. There are visual representations of hell and heaven; there are prayers to and for the dead; there are eulogies at funerals in which the blissful condition of the dead is at least mentioned and sometimes depicted in detail. Heaven (and hell) seem to cry out for depiction, and sometimes even for narrative representation.[9] But the argument to this point has been that, while Ludwig Wittgenstein was incorrect to say that death is not an event in life because it is not lived through,[10] it must nonetheless be correct to say that in so far as the event that is the completion of a human life (leaving aside the question of whether this completion is identical with physical death) is lived through, this is done with no further *telos*, and so without the possibility of being narrated. Does it then follow that the rich panoply of Christian representations of the life of the world to come (consider Dante) is just a mistake? Ought our representations of this matter be so chastened that we place shackles upon the pious practices or imaginings of Christians that have to do with their own deaths and those of their beloveds? Must, as is too often the case, the theologian with a taste for abstraction and an awareness of the tendencies of the imagination to manufacture idols, chastise the devout for the crudities of their piety?

Carol Zaleski has recently argued, in a theologically subtle and stylistically elegant book, that such a radical constraint upon the eschatological imagination would be disastrous for the practice of Christianity, and for human flourishing in general.[11] She pleads for the preservation and development of imaginatively rich conceptions of the life of the world to come on the ground that Christians need and must deploy symbols of immortality if we are to have a sense of a wider context than that bounded by the horizons of physical birth and physical death, and that such a sense is essential for the development of the virtue of hope and of a fruitful and properly Christian orientation to the goods of this sublunary world.[12] An objection to symbols of immortality, she says, would also be an objection to the use of any and all symbols for the divine in the Christian life, and would thus be a return to the heresy of the iconoclasts.[13] Much of Zaleski's argument is correct, and importantly so. But her analysis needs to be pressed further if it is to yield helpful answers to the question of this essay; if she is right that we Christians need symbolic representations of what follows the completion of a human life (and she is), it still needs to be asked how best to characterize the nature of those representations, how best to discriminate acceptable from unacceptable symbolic representations, and whether there are any appropriate nonsymbolic characterizations of the matter. That is, if Zaleski's contention about the necessity of the eschatological imagination is to be accepted, it still needs to be asked how that imagination can function properly if narrative representation is proscribed.

Two key points are needed to develop Zaleski's analysis. The first is that not all representation of what follows the completion of an individual's life need be symbolic: those events may also be characterized formally. The second is that even those representations that are properly thought of as symbolic in Zaleski's sense (she uses a blend of Paul Tillich's and Paul Ricoeur's analyses of the symbol) must eschew narrative symbolization;[14] and that, therefore, a better category for exploring the possibilities of non-narrative and non-formal representations of the life of the world to come is the icon rather than the symbol.[15]

First, on formal characterizations of the life of the world to come. Christians have developed such characterizations principally by negation. We have said that what follows upon the completion of a human life will be in virtually every respect profoundly different, inconceivably different, from what precedes it. We affirm that this life is (or will eventually become) embodied,[16] and that it is social in that it is constituted by relations at least with God and perhaps with other created beings. We affirm also that, because it is a completion, all the goods of this present life are brought to a proper consummation in it. But these affirmations are (or ought to be) framed and constrained by apophatic formalities, which is to say by a deep epistemic modesty. We do not know what our resurrected bodies will be like; sociality in eternity is strictly inconceivable for us, in large part because the possibility of emplotment is constitutive of our present understanding of sociality, and so the idea of a non-narratable form of sociality makes little immediate sense;[17] and we have little idea which among what now seem to us the goods of this life are in fact goods, and so also little idea of what it would mean for those that are genuine goods to be consummated.

Such apophatic formalities are entirely biblical. When questions about the particulars of the life of the world to come are pressed, the typical response is refusal, as when Jesus responds to the question about spousal relations in the resurrection by denying the applicability of the category (Luke 20:34–38), or when Paul refuses the question about the nature of the resurrected body by emphasizing its difference from the pre-resurrection body and the unknowability of the details of that difference (1 Cor. 15:36–58). In both these passages, the incomprehensibility of the particulars of the life of the world to come is emphasized principally by replacing all attempts to narrate those particulars (attempts implicit in the questions offered to Jesus and Paul) with a strictly formal characterization. Jesus contrasts the always narratable marriage customs of the children of this world with the utter absence of such narratable customs among those whose lives have been completed in the final eschaton; and this is to be read as a formal negation that denies a particular narratable property (and by implication all such properties) to the resurrected. Similarly, Paul offers a series of formal negations as a means of contrasting resurrected bodies with our bodies. The former are of a different sort than the latter, but this difference is explained formally by listing the properties of the latter and then negating them (earthly/heavenly, corruptible/incorruptible, dishonorable/glorious, weak/strong, natural/spiritual, and so forth). But he is willing to offer neither a narrated nor a substantively positive account of what the resurrected body will be like; this, he says, is a mystery best characterized as consisting in radical and incomprehensible change (1 Cor. 15:51).[18]

Final eschatology in the mode of apophatic formality is, therefore, one way in which the unnarratable life of the world to come can (and must, if idolatry is to be restrained) be represented. But even formal negations can represent that with which their negations have to do in another mode, a mode best understood as iconic. Consider Paul's fine words, *blepomen gar arti di'esoptrou en ainigmati, tote de prosopon pros prosopon; arti ginosko ek merous, tote de epignosomai kathos kai epegnosthen* (1 Cor. 13:12)—"For now we see enigmatically, through a mirror, but then we shall see face to face; now I know partially, but then I will fully know as I have been fully known."[19] These words are explicit in their assertion of the necessity of deep epistemic modesty with respect to matters of final eschatology, as also in their formal assertion that the life of the world to come (*arti–tote*, now–then) will be the completion (fulfilment, consummation) of life now (*ginosko–epignosomai*, I know–I will fully know), a condition in which epistemic modesty will no longer be necessary. They imply, too, in their use of the figure of the mirror to characterize our present state, a reflection of our gaze back to ourselves by something finite, something not God, something that is an idol. We look and we do not see God; we see only a half-understood, shadowy image that, if taken to be God, becomes an idol. This preliminary and premature reflection of our gaze back to ourselves is characteristic of the inevitably idolatrous tendencies of our perceptions and judgments now, but not then; then, we shall see God directly; our gaze will not be reflected back to us by anything other than God.

Substantively, Paul's sentence says almost nothing about the nature or particulars of the life of the world to come. But it can be more than an assertion of the necessity of apophatic formalities; it can be an icon, a sign of that about which it speaks in which attentive readers (or hearers) can find their understanding of the life of the world to come addressed by and conformed to precisely the God in relation with whom that life will be lived. In the interpretation briefly sketched in the preceding paragraph, I have already begun to treat it as such, as a form of words that permits the eye or the ear to take it not as an idol, a fixed, exhausted object, limited by its lineaments, but rather as an icon whose mode of being is not exhausted or fixed or frozen by being heard (or read), but which points to (suggests, evokes, provokes) something strictly inexhaustible, which is God and our eternal praise of him in the life of the world to come. Through this verbal icon, God gazes at us and leads our gaze toward (though does not bring it to) the completion of our lives in the life of the world to come.[20]

The point of these all-too-brief remarks about apophatic formalities and icons has been to suggest two things. First, that what Zaleski advocates as rich imaginative conceptions of the life of the world to come are better (and more precisely) understood as iconic representations, representations (in word, music, or image) by means of which God addresses us and directs our understanding and our vision toward the eternal future of our worshipful return to him of what he has given (and gives and will give) to us—toward (without ever reaching), that is to say, our final eschaton. Second, that the proper concepts for thinking about final individual eschatology should themselves be iconic, which means at least that they should serve recursively to remove their own tendencies to become fixed, immovable items (idols) in the conceptual furniture of our understanding.[21] Christians, therefore, ought to represent human life after completion only by icons, some strictly conceptual and some imagistic.

There is neither space nor occasion here for a full characterization of the iconic. I can note only that although an icon must have material or rhetorical properties of a certain sort, the presence of these will not guarantee its status as iconic. The property *being an icon* is therefore not without remainder an aesthetic property, nor one whose presence or absence can be decisively ascertained by the work of the critic. Ordered complexity in a certain degree, whose presence can be so ascertained, must no doubt be possessed by anything with claim to be called beautiful, and may suffice to make what possesses it beautiful. But icons, although they must be beautiful (and therefore must be complexly ordered) are not made iconic just by being beautiful. Rather, *being an icon* is a property constituted also indexically and relationally. Your icon may be my idol; my idol may be your icon; what was once my idol might become my icon. This is obvious, I take it, from the fact that it is possible to treat the words of the Bible or the teachings of the Church either iconically or with idolatry (though much more would have to be said than I can say here in order to give a sense of what treating them in either way would mean). An icon is always such for a particular person or group at a time and in a place (hence indexicality), and is always such in virtue of the relations it is instrumental in establishing between acts of human understanding and the reality of God (hence relationality).

It follows that in saying that Christian representations (whether conceptual or linguistic) of the life of the world to come should always be iconic, I raise the empirical question of whether the concepts that order the representations of this matter that we most commonly use (heaven, hell, the kingdom of God, eternal life, the resurrection of the body) are in fact at the moment usually iconic for Christians. I rather doubt that they are, though it is always very difficult to tell in any particular instance of their use just how they are being used. A half-awareness of the non- or anti-iconic use of such representations is a partial explanation of the contemporary uneasiness on the part of many theologians about such representations, and their resulting attempts to restrain and constrain their use in popular piety, and to interpret them in such a way that they need not imply idolatry or suggest excessively detailed claims to knowledge in the sphere of final eschatology.[22]

The main problem, I suspect, is that we Christians narrativize our final-eschatological representations too quickly and too easily, and in so doing turn them into idols. We improperly extend the sense we have of our own identity here below, a sense unavoidably given to us narratively, into the life of the world to come, and end by asking questions of the same kind as those asked of Jesus by the Sadducees. Shall I see my dead father again? Will I be reconciled with my estranged child? Will my beloved dog and I be reunited? Shall I have in heaven the healthy body that I had at twenty, or the decayed and painful one I have now, at eighty? Such questions, familiar to those who deal pastorally with bereavement and approaching death, are almost unavoidably idolatrous.[23] Taking them as questions that we might be able to answer freezes the gaze upon an idolatrous narrative, and prevents the gaze from being led toward God's deep mercies, which will in fact complete us by lifting us out of the realm of narrative into that of unnarratable eternity.

These idolatrous tendencies are in large part suggested to us by the very force of our narrative of God's creative and redemptive activity. We constantly tell and retell that story, so that it is written on our bodies as much as on our minds and hearts, and so that we begin to forget how to represent our faith to ourselves non-narratively (whether formally or iconically). We become compulsive singers of our tale, to the point where we forget that God's gift to us is not exhaustively constituted by the tale we sing (the tale has both *incipit* and *explicit*; God has neither), but always precedes, exceeds, and supersedes it. The liturgy, properly understood and participated in, reminds us of the limits of narrative as a representation of the content of faith;[24] so also do some of the conceptual resources of the faith and some of its literary forms. Among the former I have in mind the doctrine of the immanent Trinity, with its iconic presentation of the eternal and ceaseless exchange of gifts among the persons of the Trinity. And among the latter I have in mind the *carmina catenata* (chained poems) of John Donne and George Herbert, in which the last line of each stanza is the first line of the next, and the last line of the entire poem is also its first, with the result that the reading of the poem never ceases.[25] Such poems have no *telos* other than the continuous fact of being read; in this they iconically represent the life of the world to come, which likewise has no *telos* other than the ceaseless receiving of gifts from God and returning them to God.

But nonetheless, Christian resources for nonidolatrous representation of the life of the world to come stand in some need of renewal. We Christians have traditionally often looked outside the bounds of the Christian tradition for resources (conceptual and practical) when needs of this sort have become apparent. The Egyptians (a traditional type of the religious alien), Christians have often thought, possess resources of value for Christian purposes, gold that we can use to ornament the ark of the covenant.[26] When we find it—and because of the omnivorous nature of Christian thought we ought ceaselessly to be looking for it—we can and should appropriate (expropriate) it for our own constructive purposes. In so doing, of course, we are likely to transform it so that it becomes largely unrecognizable to those who originally mined and shaped it, just as women taken in war are to be transformed before they can be bedded, according to the Deuteronomic regulations on the matter.[27] In this spirit, I shall conclude this essay by asking what resources one group of contemporary Egyptians—the Buddhists—might have to offer on this matter. Is there anything in Buddhist thought that might serve Christians as an iconic representation of their own end, as an icon of narrative closure that is not simple cessation?

Nirvana as Icon of the End

Nirvana, a Sanskrit word with an etymology that suggests "blowing out" (of a candle flame) or "extinction" (of a fire), has been naturalized into English since the nineteenth century with a wide range of meanings, including "final beatitude", "heaven", and "blissful ecstasy". It (and its translational equivalents in other Buddhist languages) was a central technical term in Buddhist systematic thought, a frequent object of representation in Buddhist art (as a city, a lake, a tower, an empty circle, and so on), and a device for providing an end to Buddhist narratives, most especially the narrative of the Buddha, which ends with his (physical) death, characterized as entry into Nirvana, his being "nirvanized" in such a way that there are no more stories to tell about him, and no possibility of further interaction with him, as a living human being walking the earth.[28] "Nirvana" has had a range of meanings and a kind of significance for Buddhists reasonably comparable with (and probably greater than) those of "heaven" for Christians. It would therefore be absurd to attempt a survey of the range of the term's uses and the meanings attributed to it. Instead, I'll offer an interpretation of the term's principal syntactic uses within the broad framework of (Indian) Buddhist thought and practice.[29] However, the interpretation offered, brief, schematic, and partial as it must be, is not intended primarily as a tool to permit better understandings of Buddhism (though it can be so used), but rather as an icon that may be of use to Christian thinkers for the purposes already mentioned.

Buddhist systematic thought presents each person's history as beginningless, though as capable of coming to an end.[30] Until the end comes (if it does), every moment of these infinitely many human histories is characterized, always and necessarily, by ignorance (*avidyā*) of the true state of the universe and of the place within it of the particular history to which it belongs; by a complex of passionate attachment to (*rāga*), aversion from (*dveṣa*), and confusion about (*moha*) the particular things with which it has been, is, or may be in causal contact; and by an unremitting unsatisfactoriness or unpleasantness (*duḥkha*).[31] Further, each event in this history is transient, or impermanent (*anitya*), rapidly and inevitably ceasing to be just what it is and becoming something else. This beginningless progression of impermanence is punctuated by death, again and again (*punarmr.tyu*), each death being a prelude to a new birth and a subsequent death. The principle forces perpetuating this beginningless continuum are passionate desire for more of precisely those things intrinsic to it (food, sex, wealth, power, status, reputation), and deep ignorance about the true nature of this desire and its effects. Specifying the best way to think about the relation between these two (desire and ignorance) is one of the main tasks of Buddhist philosophical psychology.

Given the understanding of narrative in play in this essay, the events of any particular human history (or of the collectivity of all human histories) cannot, on the view of them given in the preceding paragraph, be narrated. This is because they cannot be emplotted: there is no progression, no *telos*, no possibility of completion or truncation, no sense of an ending. Instead, there is only infinitely more of the same, a beginningless and endless series that can be represented annalistically, logged, recorded, enumerated, listed, checked off—but not narrated. The icon of Nirvana is what, for Buddhist thought, makes narrative possible. It is what comes at the end, what marks the ending, and thereby what permits the transformation of an annal into a narrative. It can do this because, formally, it is defined consistently as the absence of all the marks by which the beginningless series is understood and defined. It is the absence of greed, hatred, and delusion; the absence of ignorance; the end of death (and so also of birth); the replacement of unsatisfactoriness with its contradictory, which is delight and bliss (*ānanda, sukha*); and the transformation of impermanence into permanence (*nityatā*). When Gautama Śākyamuni, the Buddha for our world and time, enters Nirvana (is nirvanized, *parinivṛta*), this is what happens to him: this is the culmination of his history, as it is also the potential culmination of each of ours. It is what makes it possible to tell his story—or, more precisely, it is the condition of the possibility of his having a story at all, rather than only a sequence without end or beginning.

Formal negations of the kind mentioned in the preceding paragraph are quite central to Buddhist representations of Nirvana, though Buddhists do not (any more than Christians) limit their representations of the culmination of individual life to these apophatic formalities. Nirvana is also represented in iconic images (verbal and visual) as the perfect city, the extinction of a blazing fire, the bottomless ocean, the perfect sun, the full moon, and so on.[32] But images, and the conventions governing their presentation and appropriation, are unlike apophatic formalities in having deep and very particular cultural roots; they cannot easily or quickly be transported from one master text to another, and if the deployment of Buddhist iconic images for Nirvana is a possibility for Christians at all, within the syntactic and semantic bounds of the Christian master text, this will happen only after they have been read into the Christian account, inscribed into its margins, by the kind of deep reading mentioned at the beginning of this essay. That is a long and difficult process, and not one even to sketch the lineaments of here.

It is easier with apophatic formalities: that kind of Egyptian gold requires less hard work in the smithy to make it suitable for the ornamentation of the ark. For the Buddhist master text, then, we can say that whatever properties are predicated of human existence without Nirvana are negated of such existence within Nirvana. This is a familiar move: it does for Buddhists syntactically exactly what (for example) Paul's characterization of the resurrected body does for Christians. For Paul, the resurrected body is represented formally by predicating of it the contradictories of all those properties that belong to the pre-resurrection body. For the Buddhist master text, Nirvana as the end (culmination) of life can be represented formally by predicating of it the contradictories of all those properties that belong to unnirvanized human history. Syntactically, the result is the same: the marking of an end, and the concomitant opening of a space into which systematic thought can make no further incursions without producing aporias.[33]

This is not, of course, to say that the formal characterization which Christians do (or should) give to the life of the world to come is in every respect identical to that given by Buddhists to Nirvana. These formal characterizations are identical only in the syntactic senses mentioned; in every other they are deeply different. The most important differences are given by the differences (incompatibilities) in the substantive content of what is negated in each case. Most basically, the Buddhist master text negates properties that belong to a sequence without beginning, while the Christian master text negates properties that belong to one with beginning. This means that, without Nirvana, human histories as understood by Buddhism can only terminate or continue indefinitely: neither truncation nor completion is possible for them. But for Christianity, even without the completion of the life of the world to come, truncation is possible, and termination is not. From this deep syntactic difference stem the many more particular differences in what is negated.

Nonetheless, the syntax of the Buddhist master text is, by and large, clearer than that of the Christian one in this matter of apophatic formality, and as a result it may serve as a usable conceptual icon for Christians in thinking about (and seeing through) our own characterizations of the life of the world to come. Conceptually (formally), the principal temptation for Christians with respect to making claims about the life of the world to come has been (and remains) that of saying too much in a narrative way, of not being clear about the necessity for epistemic modesty and for taking the silence produced by such modesty as an opportunity rather than a problem.

Consider the following four negations as a potential conceptual icon of the life of the world to come: (i) it is not the case that the resurrected body exists; (ii) it is not the case that the resurrected body does not exist; (iii) it is not the case that the resurrected body both exists and does not exist; (iv) it is not the case that the resurrected body neither exists nor does not exist. This is a version of the Buddhist tetralemma (*catuṣkoṭi*), a set of alternatives designed to delineate and then to negate all the possible conceptual alternatives in thinking about whether a particular predicate (in this case "exists") can be applied to a particular subject (in this case "the resurrected body").[34] Some aporias result (or they may), but it is not the burden of this essay to pursue them. Rather, the point is that this fourfold set of negations can be iconic, a representation through which God gazes at us and leads our gaze toward him without freezing it upon some representation which is other than him— upon an idol. This is not, of course, how the Buddhist master text uses this fourfold set semantically; but it is not far from its use of these negations syntactically, since one of the subjects to which the fourfold negation is applied is the existence of the Buddha after he has entered Nirvana (become nirvanized).

It might be objected that Christians ought to say that the second of the four alternatives given in the preceding paragraph is the true one. But, as is implied by what has already been said about apophatic formalities, the verb "to exist" cannot be applied univocally to the body I have now and the body I shall have then. One of the iconic functions of the tetralemma as applied to the resurrected body, then, is that it prevents (or suggests the possibility of preventing) the freezing of the conceptual gaze upon the predicate "exists" with respect to the resurrected body, and as a result checks (or might check) the temptation to construct narratives about the career of that body.

Expropriating this tetralemma from its Buddhist context and making it into a Christian icon for the life of the world to come is best thought of as providing a new illuminated decoration in the margin of the sacred page.[35] Decorating the sacred page in ways such as this is among the most exciting and challenging tasks for Christian theology in the immediate future, an essential part of coming to understand better how to represent iconically what cannot be represented discursively. And while this essay has self-consciously avoided treating transitional eschatology, including every variety of chiliasm, it may not be inappropriate to end with the pious (but sapiential)[36] hope that the new millennium, now beginning, may be characterized by increasing effort on the part of Christian theologians, as our knowledge of the particulars of the thought and practice of religious aliens increases, to use Egyptian gold to decorate the sacred page more lavishly and to ornament the ark of the covenant more gorgeously.

NOTES

1   Thanks for comments and suggestions are due to K. Beise, J. Buckley, J. Heyhoe, D. Jeffreys, J. Walls, and C. Zaleski.

2   Following Frank Kermode's fine phrase in *The Sense of an Ending: Studies in the Theory of Fiction* (Oxford: Oxford University Press, 1966), p. 45.

3 Hayden White, *The Content of the Form: Narrative Discourse and Historical Representation* (Baltimore, MD: Johns Hopkins University Press, 1987), p. 6.

4 Wolfhart Pannenberg has some interesting and entirely correct observations on the necessarily metaphorical nature of the apocalyptic language used in what I am calling transitional eschatology. See *Systematische Theologie*, Band III (Göttingen, 1993), pp. 667–668 = *Systematic Theology*, Vol. 3 (Grand Rapids, MI: Wm. B. Eerdmans Publishing Company, 1998), pp. 621–622.

5 It's not clear how best to understand *bereshith*. Better might be, "As [God] was beginning ...". See the texts translated in A. J. Rosenberg, *Genesis, A New English Translation: Translation of Text, Rashi, and Other Commentators* (New York, NY: Judaica Press, 1993), pp. 2–7.

6 On these syntactic points I have been influenced by (and largely follow) Hans Urs von Balthasar's *Was dürfen wir hoffen?* (Einsiedeln, 1986), trans. David Kipp and Lothar Krauth in *Dare We Hope "That All Men Be Saved"?* (San Francisco, CA: Ignatius Press, 1988).

7 There are some obvious exceptions to this principle for Catholic and Orthodox Christians, at least with respect to people who have died (Mary and the saints). Perhaps there are none for at least some Protestant Christians.

8 I follow Jürgen Moltmann here in emphasizing the life of the world to come as a new beginning. For Moltmann, Christian eschatology has not to do with ends or last things, but rather with new beginnings, just as the "end" of Christ was his resurrection. Moltmann is worried about the diversion of interest and attention from the exercise of our historically situated and narratable freedom that may result from thinking about eschatology as the end of history, time, and narrative. But no such diversion need result; the key point, that eschatology must involve thought about the end of narratable time, is acknowledged by Moltmann, for example in *Das Kommen Gottes: Christliche Eschatologie* (Gütersloh, 1995), p. 12 = *The Coming of God: Christian Eschatology* (Minneapolis, MN: Fortress Press, 1996), p. xi. His further claim that the eschaton of individuals must be thought of as the "Anfang der ewigen Geschichte des Lebens" can be accepted so long as "Geschichte" does not involve or require narratable sequence (as "ewige" suggests that it may not).

9 For histories of such representations see: Colleen McDannell and Bernhard Lang, *Heaven: A History* (New Haven, CT: Yale University Press, 1988); Jeffrey Burton Russell, *A History of Heaven: The Singing Silence* (Princeton, NJ: Princeton University Press, 1997).

10 "Der Tod is kein Ereignis des Lebens. Den Tod erlebt man nicht." Ludwig Wittgenstein, *Tractatus Logico-Philosophicus*, 6.431.

11 Carol Zaleski, *The Life of the World to Come: Near-Death Experience and Christian Hope* (New York, NY: Oxford University Press, 1996).

12 Zaleski, *Life*, p. 28 and passim, has some useful and penetrating things to say about the strictly evocative function of eschatological symbols.

13 Zaleski, *Life*, pp. 34–35.

14 It might seem that my emphasis upon the rejection of narrative representation runs counter to Zaleski's interest in the narratives of near-death experience, evident both in *Life* and in her earlier work, *Otherworld Journeys: Accounts of Near-Death Experience in Medieval and Modern Times* (New York, NY: Oxford University Press, 1987). But I do not think that it does; those matters have to do with what I am calling transitional eschatology rather than with final eschatology, and narrative is perfectly appropriate for the representation of transitional eschatology—though even there Pannenberg's aforementioned emphasis upon the importance of understanding (transitional) eschatological language as metaphorical should be taken to heart.

15 These points (to be developed below) are intended only in friendly amendment to and development of Zaleski's argument.

16 The parenthetical phrase is intended to preserve neutrality on the complex question of an intermediate (embodied? disembodied?) state between physical death and final resurrection. Peter van Inwagen's recent philosophical and exegetical arguments to the effect that Christians need believe neither in such an intermediate state nor in a disembodied state are powerful. See his *The Possibility of Resurrection and Other Essays in Christian Apologetics* (Boulder, CO: Westview Press, 1998), pp. 45–67. These arguments may usefully be compared with a now widely-canvassed theological position, developed from that enunciated by Benedict XII in 1336 in the Bull *Benedictus Deus*, to the effect that entry into eternity follows for every individual immediately upon death (animae sanctorum omnium ... mox

post mortem suam ... etiam ante resumptionem suorum corporum et iudicium generale post ascensionem Salvatoris Domini nostri Iesu Christi in caelum, fuerunt, sunt, et erunt in caelo, caelorum regno et paradiso caelesti cum Christo ..., Denzinger-Schönmetzer, p. 1000; with the same rapidity but different particulars those who die in mortal sin enter upon their eternal destiny). On this see Joseph Ratzinger, *Eschatologie Tod und ewiges Leben* (Regensburg, 1977), pp. 91–135 = *Eschatology: Death and Eternal Life* (Washington, DC: Catholic University Press of America, 1988), pp. 104–161; Pannenberg, *Systematische Theologie*, Band III, pp. 641–654 = *Systematic Theology*, Vol. 3, pp. 577–580; Moltmann, *Kommen Gottes*, pp. 74–96 = *Coming of God*, pp. 58–77.

17   On the strict unimaginability of personal immortality see, convincingly, Bernard Williams, "The Makropulos Case: Reflections on the Tedium of Immortality", in idem, *Problems of the Self: Philosophical Papers 1956–1972* (Cambridge: Cambridge University Press, 1973), pp. 82–100.

18   Paul exhibits a similar epistemic modesty with respect to what he can properly say about his experience of being "caught up into paradise" (2 Cor. 12:1–7).

19   Compare the use of the mirror-image in a reversed sense in 2 Cor. 3:18, and Jean-Luc Marion's comments thereon in *Dieu sans l'être: Hors-texte* (Paris, 1982), pp. 34–35 = *God Without Being: Hors-Texte* (Chicago, IL: University of Chicago Press, 1991), pp. 21–22.

20   In this sketchy characterization of the iconic I rely upon Marion, *Dieu sans l'être*, pp. 15–37 = *God Without Being*, pp. 7–24; and Pavel Florensky, *Iconostasis* (Crestwood, NJ: St. Vladimir's Seminary Press, 1996), especially pp. 44–68. The deeper background to Florensky's treatment of icons is in his *The Pillar and Ground of the Truth* (Princeton, NJ: Princeton University Press, 1996). Donald Davidson's analysis of metaphor, found in "What Metaphors Mean", *Critical Inquiry* 5 (1978), pp. 31–47, has some deep analogies (though couched in a very different idiom) to Marion's (and to a lesser extent Florensky's) analysis of the icon.

21   Poetic representation of such recursively deconstructive tendencies can be seen in many of George Herbert's poems. See, e.g., "The Altar". Stanley Fish is good on this aspect of Herbert. See his *Self-Consuming Artifacts: The Experience of Seventeenth-Century Literature* (Berkeley, CA: University of California Press, 1972); *The Living Temple: George Herbert and Catechizing* (Berkeley, CA: University of California Press, 1978).

22   Such uneasiness is among the motivations for Karl Rahner's influential theory about how eschatological assertions should be interpreted. See his "Theologische Prinzipien der Hermeneutik eschatologischer Aussagen", in *Schriften zur Theologie*, Band IV (Einsiedeln, 1960), pp. 401–428 = "The Hermeneutics of Eschatological Assertions", in *Theological Investigations*, Volume IV (Baltimore, MD: Helicon Press, 1966), pp. 323–346. But Rahner's view, which is that eschatological statements can be established solely by a method of extrapolation from what is implied by the present self-knowledge of Christians, and that the content of what little eschatological knowledge we have is just and only what knowledge of the future is needed for the present self-understanding of Christians (see his fourth thesis), goes too far. Rather, eschatology has as its primary content what God will do; and its theses are established not only by appeal to present self-understanding in Christ, but also by attention to what God has done and is doing by way of making that future present. On this see Pannenberg, *Systematische Theologie*, Band III, pp. 585–587 = *Systematic Theology*, Vol. 3, pp. 543–544.

23   Of course it does not follow from the fact that such questions are typically idolatrous that indicating this is always the proper thing to do, pastorally speaking. Better to turn the questioner's attention toward the potentially iconic representations of comfort to be found in the Church's prayers and lamentations, and most especially those found in the Psalms.

24   Liturgical reform sometimes forgets this, smoothing out the iconically repetitive moments of the Eucharistic celebration—moments in which what is done is done again, in a liturgical stammer of repeated approach to and withdrawal from God, repeated reception of God's gift and return of that gift to the giver, in an iconic representation-in-action of the life of the world to come—in the interests of providing a smooth narrative curve to the celebration. On this, see Catherine Pickstock, *After Writing: On the Liturgical Consummation of Philosophy* (Oxford: Blackwell Publishers, 1998).

25   See, *inter alia*, Donne's "La Corona" (an icon of salvation), and Herbert's "Sinnes Round" (an icon of damnation). See also Henri de Lubac, *The Christian Faith: An Essay on the*

Structure of the Apostles' Creed, trans. Richard Arnandez (San Francisco, CA: Ignatius Press, 1986), pp. 245–246, on the Apostles' Creed as a circle whose end requires a new start at its beginning—something very close to a *carmen catenatum*, though de Lubac does not use the phrase.

26   The metaphor of Egyptian gold is derived from patristic exegesis of Exodus 3:22; 11:2; 12:35–36; 25:1–7; 32:1–4; 35:4–9, 20–29. See, *inter alia*, Origen's letter to Gregory, Migne, *Patrologia Graecae*, vol. 11, cols. 86–92, translated in vol. X of the *Ante-Nicene Christian Library*, pp. 388–390; Augustine, *De doctrina christiana*, ii.60.

27   See, e.g., Jerome, Epistle 70, Migne, *Patrologiae Latinae*, vol. 22, cols. 664–668, especially 666 (discussing Deut. 21:10–14).

28   There are scholastic difficulties here with the differences between *nirvāṇa* and *parinirvāṇa* (for an excellent discussion of which based on Pali materials see Steven Collins, *Nirvana and Other Buddhist Felicities: Utopias of the Pali Imaginaire* [Cambridge: Cambridge University Press, 1998], pp. 147–151, 191–198); a partial parallel in Indian scholastic thought is the distinction between the removal of the *kleśāvaraṇāni* (affective obstacles) and that of the *jñeyāvaraṇāni* (obstacles to what needs to be known), on which see Paul J. Griffiths *et al.*, *The Realm of Awakening: A Translation and Study of Chapter Ten of Asanga's Mahāyānasangraha* (New York, NY: Oxford University Press, 1989), pp. 65, 75, 244–245. But it would be out of place to pursue these distinctions here. Also, to say that there is no further interaction with the Buddha after he has been nirvanized is very much to over-simplify. Indian Buddhist theorists found complicated and interesting ways of specifying the possibility of such interactions (for a presentation and discussion of which see my *On Being Buddha: The Classical Doctrine of Buddhahood* (Albany, NY: State University of New York Press, 1994). But these conceptual moves do not call into question the claim that Nirvana ends the narrative of the Buddha.

29   Among primary sources I have drawn mostly upon the discussions in Vasubandhu's *Abhidharmakośa* and its commentaries, ed. Dwarikadas Shastri, *Abhidharmakośa and Bhāṣya of Ācārya Vasubandhu and Sphuṭārthā Commentary of Ācārya Yaśomitra* (Varanasi: Bauddhabharati, 1981), especially i.4–6, vi.67–75. The analysis in Nāgārjuna's *Mūladmadhyamakākarikā*, together with Candrakirti's *Prasannapadā*, ed. Louis de La Vallée Poussin, *Madhyamakavṛtti: Mūlamadhyamakākārikās (Mādhyamika-sūtras) de Nāgārjuna avec la Prasannapadā, commentaire de Candrakirti* (St. Petersburg, 1913), especially ch. xxv, provides a good example of the provision of a pattern of argument that could itself be used as a conceptual icon.

30   The history of the universe is also beginningless; there is, strictly speaking, no such thing as a Buddhist cosmogony. But in accord with the limitations of this essay, I shall restrict the remarks that follow to the implications of the conceptual icon of Nirvana for individual final eschatology. There are implications for universal eschatology, too, but they are beyond my scope here.

31   This diagnosis is of course not limited to human histories but to all those that involve sentience. There are difficult and interesting questions about the limits of sentience here, on which see Lambert Schmithausen, *The Problem of the Sentience of Plants in Buddhism* (Tokyo: International Institute for Buddhist Studies, 1991).

32   The best treatments of these and other images are in Steven Collins, *Nirvana*, and in the same author's earlier work, *Selfless Persons: Imagery and Thought in Theravāda Buddhism* (Cambridge: Cambridge University Press, 1982). Interesting comparisons may be made with standard similes for Buddha's action, given at length in E. H. Johnston, ed., *The Ratnagotravibhāga Mahāyānottaratantraśtra* (Patna: Bihar Research Society, 1950), pp. 102–110. See my discussion in *On Being Buddha*, ch. 4

33   Much of the history of western attempts to interpret Buddhist representations of Nirvana have been marked by an attempt to resolve conceptual aporias without realizing that the representations are to be taken iconically. See Collins, *Nirvana*, for this point in different language. An entrée into the history of western interpretation may be had from Guy Richard Welbon, *The Buddhist Nirvana and its Western Interpreters* (Chicago, IL: University of Chicago Press, 1968).

34   There is a substantial literature on the *catuṣkoṭi*. A beginning may be made with David Seyfort Ruegg, "The Uses of the Four Positions of the Catuṣkoṭi and the Problem of the Description of Reality in Mahāyāna Buddhism", *Journal of Indian Philosophy* 5 (1977), pp. 1–71.

35 Buddhists may, of course, do something entirely similar with Christian materials for their own purposes (I hope that they will: what could be more interesting?), but only those engaged in constructive work within the bounds of the Buddhist master text have the right and the duty to do it and to say how it should go.
36 "Ecce pietas est sapientia", Augustine, *Confessiones*, v. 5.

CHAPTER 3

"WHERE THEOLOGIANS FEAR TO TREAD"

AMY PLANTINGA PAUW

A Musical Analogy

In seventeenth-century Europe, before the widespread printing of music, the composer ordinarily did not write the ornamentation of a piece of music into the score, but left it up to the discretion of the performer. This did not mean that ornamentation, particularly in slow movements, was an optional practice. It was clearly expected as an enhancement of the written notes, and in some cases the hearers judged the performance of a musical piece to a fair extent by the magnificence and tastefulness of the ornamentation. Some ornaments were rather modest, a turn or a trill, some more wide-ranging and elaborate. But within conventions of musical good taste, which varied by place and time, the performer of soloistic music could, and was expected to, exercise some imagination and freedom beyond the specifications of the musical "text".[1]

I propose the practice of Baroque musical ornamentation as an analogy to the place of reflection on angels and demons in Christian theology. It is not the main melody, but functions to enhance the main theological themes— God, creation, Christ, salvation, eschatology, and so on. My theological proposal argues against making the ministry of angels or the struggle against evil principalities and powers the center of the redemptive drama. On the other hand, the analogy to musical ornamentation suggests that reflection on angels and demons is not only appropriate, but in some cases required as a theological exercise. There is a certain constricted and unimaginative quality about theologies which refuse to leave the safety of the established melody to address the realm of the "things invisible". Like Baroque musical performance, the practice of theology requires some willingness to engage the conventional demands of the art form. Reflection on angels and demons,

Amy Plantinga Pauw
Louisville Presbyterian Theological Seminary, Louisville, KY 40205-1798, USA

however, like the practice of ornamentation, leaves considerable room for theological freedom and innovation. Lack of uniformity is intrinsic to proper performance.

This notion of reflections on angels and demons as variegated enhancements of the major melodies of faith seems to fit well with the practice of biblical writers. Angels and demons appear frequently in Scripture, without argument or fanfare, but they usually function more as stagehands than as major characters. Their task is to set the scene for the main action. When, for example, Jesus says to Simon Peter, "Satan has demanded to sift all of you like wheat, but I have prayed for you that your own faith may not fail" (Luke 22:31), the major themes for theological reflection are not the power and character of the devil, but the loving intercessions of Christ and the perils of faithful discipleship. When the angel of the Lord finds Hagar in the wilderness (Gen. 16:7–13), and issues in his own name both the command to return to her mistress Sarai and the promise of the birth of Ishmael, the dominant theological melody is the complex interplay between God's readiness to "hear" the voice of the oppressed, and what seems to be God's willingness to reinforce standing social arrangements; the angel's transparency to divine presence is a fascinating ornament to the story. Angels and demons never appear to be the main point for faith to grasp. When John in Revelation 19 falls down to worship an angel, the scandalized angel gives him a quick catechism lesson: "You must not do that! I am a fellow servant with you and your comrades who hold the testimony of Jesus. Worship God!" (Rev. 19:10).

These scriptural patterns support my constructive proposal to judge theological performance in this area not in its own right, but by how it enhances major themes such as God, human existence, redemption in Christ, and, perhaps especially, eschatology. Starting in the intertestamental period, the escalating theological attention to angels and demons placed them within the framework of a dramatic apocalyptic eschatology. This framework of ultimate judgment carried into most theological treatments, in which there is no ambiguity or uncertainty about the ultimate destinies of angels and demons—their very names point to their eschatological divergence. Their various roles in the drama of human salvation—announcing, praising, comforting, punishing, tempting, afflicting—are a living out of their eschatological ends of either glory or damnation. They appear on the stage of human redemption as creaturely actors, either witnessing to God's love or despising it; but they lack the spiritual dynamism of the human players in the drama: the human realm holds no possibility of sin and alienation for angels, or of repentance and redemption for demons.[2]

As eschatological figures, angels and demons shed light back on the earthly moral struggles of human beings, and the character of good and evil. This is true even of universalistic eschatologies like Origen's, which include the demons in the promised "restoration of all things". Reflection on angels and demons can also enhance our understanding of God. As Michael Welker points out, "The doctrine of angels illumines, in its way, God's particular glory, God's particular personality, and the particular ways God takes up contact with what is creaturely, as well as the particular problems of taking up that contact."[3] Attention to the angelic realm can also disclose hidden harmonies or dissonances between major theological themes.

The analogy of angels and demons as ornaments to the main themes of theology suggests that Christian attitudes towards them should fall somewhere between naïve credulity and arrogant dismissiveness. In a perverse way, the most radical critics of Christian faith have it right. In his review "Billions and Billions of Demons", Richard Lewontin professes his faith in Carl Sagan's vision of the "social and intellectual apparatus, Science, as the only begetter of truth". He urges all reasonable people to acknowledge their existence "as material beings in a material world", and therefore "to reject irrational and supernatural explanations of the world, the demons that exist only in their imaginations". But Sagan's master narrative requires more than the rejection of demons: "That materialism is absolute, for we cannot allow a Divine Foot in the door." After all, Lewontin scoffs, "anyone who could believe in God could believe in anything".[4] By the same token, it seems a bit odd to profess belief in God while sneering at belief in other spiritual powers. As the western church experiences a popular resurgence of belief in angels, and increasingly engages other cultures and faith traditions in which belief in spirits remains strong, the expectation increases that even western theologians will exhibit some daring and inventiveness in this area.[5] Perhaps agreeing to play the dominant theological melody of God and God's creative and redemptive purposes requires some respectful engagement with a larger spiritual realm.

Friedrich Schleiermacher tried to avoid an intellectual confrontation with Christianity's cultured despisers over the notion of angels, while respecting their place in Christian liturgy and private devotion. His compromise solution was a sympathetic acknowledgement of their importance in popular Christian practice combined with a methodological determination that angels "never enter into the sphere of Christian doctrine proper".[6] Readers of high culture journals such as this one may be sorely tempted to follow Schleiermacher here. His approach would not prevent us from joining in the singing of Christmas carols, or adding a liturgical flourish to the Eucharist by celebrating it "with angels and archangels and with all the company of heaven". But it would keep angels safely out of the range of serious theological reflection.

Likewise for demons. Schleiermacher saw that it would be "inexpedient and in many ways unjustifiable to wish to banish the conception of the devil from our treasury of song".[7] No need to forbid the singing of *A Mighty Fortress is Our God*! He noted that in some forms of Christian piety the idea of the devil is "apparently indispensable, in order to make clear the positive godlessness of evil in itself, or to emphasize the fact that it is only in a higher protection that we can find help against an evil the source of whose power our will and intelligence seem unable to reach".[8] Indeed, even Jesus and the apostles, with their exemplary religious consciousness, believed in the devil. Yet Schleiermacher declared the notion of Satan "wholly problematic" when it intruded into the sphere of dogmatics.

Schleiermacher appears torn between two sound but conflicting theological instincts. The first was that the drama of the Christian experience of redemption revolves around the figure of Jesus Christ. He has the starring role. Schleiermacher saw that to give angels and the devil major roles in Christian dogmatics would be a mistake, and that he was within his theological rights to treat them as mere stagehands. This simple, unadorned presentation of main Christian themes was particularly appropriate for cultured despisers of religion, for whom elaborate, fanciful angelologies were an offense, and a hindrance to faith. For the same reason, apologetic arguments for the existence of angels and demons are inappropriate in dogmatics. "In Christian Dogmatics ... we are just as little concerned to dispute the conception of the devil as to establish it."[9] The task of theology is not to establish the existence of angelic beings by contriving arguments that would convince the skeptics in Schleiermacher's day, or in ours. If apologetic arguments have a place in Christian theology, it is only with regard to the main themes; finer points of theological ornamentation can be dispensed with. The strategy of trying to show that angels are the one and only reality that can explain the nature of particular human experiences is doomed to failure in any case: those so inclined will always find candidates in the physical world to account for the effects attributed to angels and demons. As Goethe remarked, "Let me call nervous calm what you call an angel."[10] Angels and demons are embellishments of Christian faith, and deserve to be treated as such.

Schleiermacher's second, conflicting, theological instinct was that theology concerns the church's experience of redemption, as it is informed by the language of Scripture and communal faith. His understanding of theology made impossible a clean distinction between the experience of redemption which grounds Christian theology and ordinary Christian practice. However, the practice of ordinary Christians, from the apostles to the churchgoers of his day, was steeped in a piety that affirmed angels and demons. The idea of angels and the devil clearly *had* shaped the experience of redemption for many in the church. Thus Schleiermacher was caught between his sympathy for, and methodological dependence on, a richly ornamented communal piety and his desire to present the main points of Christian theology in a compelling and uncluttered way.

Rather than assert his right to theological freedom in this area, Schleiermacher sought refuge in a "scientific" theology that identified a basic paradigm of the Christian experience of redemption, once the elaborate and fanciful embellishments of popular religiosity were stripped away. In this paradigm, "that from which we are to be redeemed remains the same (as does the manner of our redemption) whether there be a devil or no".[11] But as Kathryn Tanner points out, this approach is problematic because "the experience of redemption in Christ in all its life-shaping implications" is by definition rooted in particular contexts. It does not "exist as some already complete whole to be simply explicated or unpacked. It does not exist as something to which the theologian can always refer back, something on which the theologian can thereby always count, to establish of itself what it is proper to say about God, the world, and the self, and those statements' relations to one another."[12]

Tanner argues that "Christian theology is not primarily placed in a high culture realm", but "has to do, instead, with the meaning dimension of Christian practices",[13] in all their historical and cultural variety. Given this construal of the theological task, the persistent appearance of angels and demons in Scripture, Christian liturgy and the popular religious imagination of Schleiermacher's day would forbid summarily dismissing this topic as superfluous to good theological performance, on the grounds that it did not belong to "scientific" theology. Instead, its prominence in communal piety would argue in favor of dogmatic attention.

On the other hand, the theological responsibility to engage the angelic realm does not in itself dictate what Schleiermacher called the theologian's "conclusion with regard to its truth".[14] The appropriateness of personifying the mysterious powers we encounter as angels and demons cannot be decided "in general". As Tanner notes about the whole process of theological production,

> Where one starts in these processes is literally a matter of where one is concretely—socially, politically, practically. It is a matter of one's very particular historical and social locations. Realistic possibilities for selection (what can be taken seriously or what is out of the question), the possible meanings of these selected materials, and what they initially seem to have to do with one another, are established in great part by the schools, churches, occupations, theological movements, and political organizations of which one is a part.[15]

With respect to angels and demons, theological conclusions about the nature of their existence will be guided by such factors as the conventions of interpreting Scripture, attitudes towards the practice of exorcism, and larger cultural assumptions about spirits that find acceptance in particular communities.

While theological reflection is always situated within a local theological culture, in the case of the "main melodies" of Christian faith there is more uniformity across different Christian cultures regarding required beliefs. While it seems pointless to practice Christian theology without belief in the existence of God and the significance of Jesus Christ, for example, this is not the case regarding belief in the existence of a personal devil. The differences of local culture may affect how directly a theologian affirms the existence of angels and demons, and to what degree they can be treated as useful, mythological personifications of radical evil and divine presence. Just as in some fast-moving Baroque pieces, ornamentation is light to non-existent, so in some arenas of theological reflection, the existence of angels and demons can remain pretty much an open question. We can grant Schleiermacher his wish not to burden his own Christian dogmatics with an elaborate angelology, as long as this theological decision is not justified on "scientific" grounds, and thereby imposed on others. In the realm of angels and demons, considerable freedom of belief and practice is to be granted, accompanied by an even greater than usual dose of theological humility.

Suppose for a variety of scriptural, societal, and practical reasons, a theologian comes to a positive conclusion regarding the truth of the existence of angels. How does this shape her theological performance? All theological construction requires imagination and strategic decisions. But in renditions of the dominant themes of theology, the theologian has more materials at hand, by way of scriptural images, creedal definitions, and traditions of theological reflection. Whatever a theologian decides to say about the realm of angels will inevitably require a creativity willing to rely far less directly on the written "score" of Scripture, liturgy, creed, and previous theological expression.[16] Gabriel Fackre remarks that

> Scripture is much more elusive, restrained, modest, and paradoxical than our aesthetic, philosophical and cultural impulses. The Bible affords no straightforward, coherent angel ontology. We learn regularly of the doing of angels, but not the details of their being.[17]

While this arguably remains true of all topics in theology, it is particularly pronounced in the case of angels and demons. Furthermore, creeds and theological traditions, which have often *not* been "elusive, restrained, modest, and paradoxical" regarding the main themes of Christian faith, have usually become so around the topic of angels and demons. Even Karl Barth counseled the "need to speak 'incidentally' and 'softly' about angels".[18]

Two Angelologies

We turn now to two bold angelologies, those of Jonathan Edwards (1703–1758) and Karl Barth (1886–1968), to test these assumptions, with a special attention to the theme of eschatology. Our function is like that of a sympathetic fellow musician, who judges the beauty and virtuosity of a colleague's performance within the aesthetic boundaries of a particular musical culture, without necessarily choosing to perform the piece the same way himself. If a theologian's rendition of angelic or demonic themes is incongruous or obtrusive, so that it detracts from the beauty of the dominant melody, it then ceases to perform its proper theological function. By contrast, a good performance imaginatively and effectively enhances the major themes of the faith. While belief in angels and a personal devil was waning among some of his day, Jonathan Edwards retained a sturdy confidence in their existence. He anchored his reflections in a third or fourth-century exegetical tradition that depicted Satan as an exalted angel who fell before the creation of the world, and a theological tradition, stretching back at least as far as Anselm of Canterbury, that saw the protological fall of Satan and his angelic followers as a depletion of the heavenly ranks that set in motion God's work of human redemption. Yet within this inherited scriptural and theological framework, he exercised considerable theological freedom.

The particular reflections under consideration were private writings, composed during the early 1740s, when Edwards was exploring "true religion" and its counterfeits for his great treatise on *Religious Affections.*[19] What Martha Nussbaum writes about the social function of Greek tragedy in ancient Athens applies to the role of Edwards' reflections on the angelic realm:

> To attend a tragic drama was not to go to a distraction or a fantasy, in the course of which one suspended one's anxious practical questions. It was, instead, to engage in a communal process of inquiry, reflection, and feeling with respect to important civic and personal ends.[20]

The first function of Edwards' reflections on angels and demons during this period was to illuminate his "anxious practical questions" about the faith struggles of earthly saints and their eschatological implications. In particular, these private entries enhanced his public reflections on the earthly dangers of spiritual pride by elaborately depicting pride's devastating consequences in the heavenly realm.

Heaven before the ascension of Christ was a spiritually perilous place, a realm of vulnerability, temptation, and uncertainty, much like Edwards' parish in Northampton, Massachusetts. " 'Tis a thing supposed without proof that the glorious inhabitants of heaven never felt any such thing as trouble or uneasiness of any kind", he declared.[21] The angels "have known what it is to be in great danger and to be distressed with fear" for their salvation. They have experienced "their own weakness and mutability and insufficiency for themselves".[22] Indeed, the residents of heaven in some ways faced a deeper spiritual struggle than the earthly saints: angels enjoyed a superior place in Edwards' hierarchically stratified cosmos, and so experienced an even greater temptation to spiritual pride, a temptation which some were able to resist, and to which some dramatically succumbed. In plumbing the religious psyches of both Satan and the elect angels, Edwards found a magnified version of the struggle against spiritual pride unfolding on earth.

For the angels, eschatological bliss and security in heaven required a humility willing to give up the superior status and dignity of heaven. The virtue of humility was, for Edwards, not cowering subservience or self-denigration, but "a grace proper for beings who are excellent and glorious beings", guided by a vision of God's supreme "loveliness".[23] Like Christ, the angels were not to count their heavenly intimacy with God as something to be grasped, but to empty themselves. The "proper business" of the angels, "the end of their creation", was "to be ministering spirits to men".[24] Christ's humility in ministering to fallen humanity was a model to angels who were tempted to spurn God's role for them in human salvation as demeaning to their dignity. Christ exemplified a love for human creatures that was willing to leave the comforts of heaven to join in God's magnificent work of redemption.

The ultimate test of the angels' faithfulness and humility was their willingness to serve and adore Christ, "in his abject meanness, and when set at naught and abased to hell for beloved though sinful, vile men".[25] Through his reflections on angels, Edwards probed what he saw as pride's natural inclination to "despise a crucified Savior, one that suffered such disgrace, and humbled himself so low".[26] The blessed angels are the ones who took no offense at God's strange work of redemption through a savior in whom "majesty and meekness" coincide. Indeed they "have the greatest manifestations of the glory of God by what they see in the work of men's redemption, and especially in the death and sufferings of Christ".[27]

There is a surprising convergence between Edwards' treatment of angelic humility and Dietrich Bonhoeffer's reflections in the second chapter of his tantalizingly sketchy "Outline for a Book":

> Encounter with Jesus Christ. The experience that a transformation of all human life is given in the fact that "Jesus is there only for others." His "being there for others" is the experience of transcendence. It is only this "being there for others", maintained till death, that is the ground of his omnipotence, omniscience, and omnipresence. Faith is participation in this being of Jesus (incarnation, cross, and resurrection). Our relation to God is not a "religious" relationship to the highest, most powerful, and best Being imaginable—that is not authentic transcendence—but our relation to God is a new life in "existence for others", through participation in the being of Jesus.[28]

Bonhoeffer then went on to wonder what it would mean to interpret biblical concepts, including "the last things", on this basis. In a way that gave free rein to his theological virtuosity; this seems to be what Edwards was doing. He let the main theme of a savior "set at naught and abased to hell" out of love for sinners guide what he imaginatively surmised about faithfulness in the heavenly realm, both in the present and eschatologically. It would be incongruous in this theological paradigm for the highest creatures of heaven to exemplify the eudaemonistic ideal of eternal, non-suffering bliss.[29] For Edwards, angelic existence was not a heavenly sinecure but a "participation in the being of Jesus".

The angels enjoyed the eschatological fulfillment of Jesus' teaching that "those who want to save their life will lose it, and those who lose their life for my sake will find it" (Matt. 16:25). Because they were willing "to perish or die as to self-dependence and all self-fullness" in serving Christ's work of redemption, in the new heaven they find themselves before "the infinite fountain of glory and love, the beholding and enjoying of which, and union with which, being the elect creature's all in all—all its strength, all its beauty, all its life, its fruit, its honor and its blessedness".[30] Heaven is no longer an insecure place, but "a world of love", in which all the angels and saints rejoice together in Christ. The angels' love for human creatures also finds its eschatological culmination. In heaven "the angels and saints all love one another ... As they are all lovely, so all see each other's loveliness with answerable delight and complacence. Everyone there loves every other inhabitant of heaven whom he sees, and so he is mutually beloved by everyone."[31] One of the angels' eschatological rewards for a humility that recognized divine loveliness and responded to the urgings of divine love is the perfection of their own love and loveliness.

I would judge Edwards' portrayal of the angels to be a beautiful enhancement of his dominant emphasis on the centrality of love and humility in the life of faith, seen above all in the person and work of Christ. The angels ornament both the divine and human sides of the work of redemption. In their ministry to human beings, the angels mirror both Christ's humility before God, and his love for humanity. In their creaturely vulnerability, they illuminate the weakness and dependence of human beings on Christ. Most importantly, they point God's dynamic work of human redemption towards its millennial harvest and eschatological end in a "world of love", in which divine glory and creaturely happiness coincide.

When Edwards turned to his imaginative depiction of the devil, his theological focus shifted from the confluence of humility and love to the connections between pride and hatred. During this period, Edwards was interested more in the character of human sin than in its origins. Thus he stressed Satan's alienation from God, not his temptations of humanity. Avoiding the common theological ploy that Bonhoeffer playfully called *diaboli ex machina*,[32] Edwards did not appeal to the devil to explain the origin of human sin; instead he used this figure to probe creaturely resistance to God's redemptive aims, and the eschatological result of this resistance.

Like Milton's portrayal of the devil in *Paradise Lost*, Edwards' Satan was an exalted figure before his fall:

for great indeed
His name, and high was his degree in Heav'n;
His count'nance, as the Morning Starr that guides
The starrie flock ...[33]

Like Milton, Edwards followed the long exegetical tradition that took Job's image of "the morning stars singing together" as a reference to the angels. Satan then becomes Lucifer, "the chief of all the angels, of greatest natural capacity, strength and wisdom, and highest in honor and dignity, the brightest of all those stars of heaven". This trope connected the fate of Satan with "what is said of him under that type of the devil, the king of Babylon: 'How art thou fallen from heaven, O Lucifer, son of the morning' ".[34] Isaiah's taunt to the king of Babylon thus became part of a cosmic story of fall and redemption.

Except that in Edwards' hands Isaiah's exclamation was less a taunt than a lament. The tradition Edwards knew pointed to Satan's prideful desire to be like God as the origin of his fall. In this way Satan became a prototype for the fall of Adam and Eve, who were also seduced by the desire to "be like God, knowing good and evil" (Gen. 3:5). Instead of adopting this tradition, Edwards boldly made Satan a prototype of Christ. "Lucifer, in having the excellency of all those glorious things that were about him all summed up in him, he was a type of Christ, in whom all the glory and excellency of all elect creatures is more properly summed [up] as the Head and Fountain of all, as the brightness of all that reflects the light of the sun is summed up in the sun." Satan was the "anointed cherub" of God, and thus, before his fall, was called "the Messiah or Christ or anointed".[35] Satan's fall was not just from creaturely greatness, but from a messianic calling.

In a striking echo of the Christological language of Colossians 1, Edwards noted that "as all the angels are all called 'the sons of God,' Lucifer was his firstborn, and was the firstborn of every creature". This meant that God appointed Satan to be "the grand minister of his providence" within the earthly realm. His calling was to reflect the loveliness of God by a ministry of love to human creatures. But this is precisely what Satan refused to do:

When it was revealed to him, that as high and as glorious as he was, that he must be a ministering spirit to the race of mankind that he had seen newly created, that appeared so feeble, mean and despicable, so vastly inferior not only to him, the prince of the angels and head of the universe, but also to the inferior angels, and that he must be subject to one of that race that should hereafter be born, he could not bear it. This occasioned his fall, and now he with other angels he drew away with him are fallen.[36]

Though Edwards' supralapsarian reference to Christ as "one of that race that should hereafter be born" confuses things a bit, his portrayal of Satan in these private entries remained decidedly Christological. The fallen Satan is truly the Antichrist in Edwards' theology, one who disdainfully rejected his own anointed role to serve God's loving intentions for "feeble, mean and despicable" humanity, and who thus could only "despise the crucified Savior".

Edwards noted the theological dissonance that Satan's fall created within the larger scheme of God's plan for human redemption:

Some may be ready to think it to be incredible, and what the wisdom of the Creator would not suffer that the most glorious of all his creatures should fall and be eternally ruined, or that it should be so that the elect angels, those that are beloved of God, should none of them be of equal strength and largeness of capacity with the devil.[37]

Despite Edwards' energetic efforts to vindicate God's wisdom in "suffering" this calamity, the fall of Satan remains incredible. How could God's anointed one, beloved of God and gifted with the highest created excellencies, refuse to reflect God's love in hospitality to others, preferring isolation and hatred? Why should the wisdom of the Creator suffer this frustration of its eschatological ends in creating the world? Despite Edwards' protestations, the fall of Satan shows the vulnerability of the divine plan to create "a world of love". Satan's cooperation in being a ministering spirit cannot be coerced, and his tragic refusal is not remedied, even in the eschaton.

Unable to accept God's goodness to weak and undeserving humans, Satan finally rejects it for himself. Marilyn Adams has described some of the dynamics of such prideful separatism in the human realm. God's

inclusion of outcasts [read *human creatures*], which is part and parcel of the policy, strikes separatists [read *Satan*] as unfair and outrageous and provokes them to exclude themselves. And God cannot demonstrate his inclusiveness toward separatists if they refuse to be included ... More than that, the persistent separatist thereby forces God to compromise his policy of inclusiveness itself: either he includes the separatist and excludes those with whom the separatist refuses to associate; or he includes the latter and the former separate themselves. In thus accepting the possibility of external separation "in the judgment," God opens himself up to a double defeat.[38]

Edwards adamantly rejected the language of divine defeat; his eschatology celebrates the triumph of the glorious power and unsearchable wisdom of God. For Edwards, the immense difficulty of the redemptive endeavor was the perfect stage for displaying God's sovereign glory. A smooth, placid affair, devoid of struggle or bitter disappointment, would not serve nearly as well. Yet his writings are full of poignant reflections on the horrible and irremediable consequences of Satan's refusal of such a magnificent calling, both for himself, and for the creaturely world as a whole.

Wendy Farley would likely deem Edwards a member of the theological tradition she calls "strenuously antitragic". Yet the contrast in her "tragic vision" between the "domination, violence and terror" characteristic of evil power and "the power of creativity, wisdom, and compassion" characteristic of good echoes Edwards' contrast between the powers of Satan and the good angels.[39] The angels' ministry of wisdom and compassion in the world reflects their vision of the complementarity of God's awesome power and loveliness. Satan and his cohorts have a fatally skewed vision of God: "they see God's awful greatness, yet they see nothing of his loveliness".[40] In Bonhoeffer's phrase, God for the demons is only "the highest, most powerful, and best Being imaginable". The power Satan relies on, as he "restlessly endeavors to set up himself in this world and maintain his dominion here",[41] is a power divorced from humility and love. Tragically, in the present age, his reign of violence and terror seems stronger than the power of goodness: much of the world is under his sway, for none of the elect angels are "of equal strength and largeness of capacity with the devil".

In the eschaton, good triumphs. Despite its most unpromising beginning, God's work of redemption is ultimately a glorious success. Christ takes Satan's place as "the bright morning star" (Rev. 22:16), and the good angels are exalted far above the devil's original stature. The angels, the saints and the Lamb revel together in an incorruptible, inexhaustible world of love, a reflection of God's perfect loveliness. The power of evil is finally vanquished in a paroxysm of apocalyptic violence. It seems to be God's awful greatness, not God's loveliness, that secures the ultimate defeat of Satan. God "gave this honor, dignity and power unto [Christ] in an infinitely higher and more glorious manner than ever he had done to Lucifer, and appointed him to conquer, subdue and execute vengeance upon that great rebel".[42] Having spurned participation in God's work of love, Satan is eternally consigned to hell, "a world of hatred", whose inhabitants "agree to nothing but hatred and expressions of hatred".[43]

Edwards' vivid contrast between Satan's exalted calling and his ignominious fall and defeat was meant to enhance his "eschatology of glory". Only a God of supreme power and wisdom could triumph in the face of these incredible setbacks. Instead, this contrast seems to mute the triumphant themes of Edwards' eschatology, by echoing Christological themes of the vulnerability of divine love. His elaborate personification of the devil as a creature who refused God's summons to "live for others" makes the victory of good over evil seem tragically incomplete rather than gloriously realized. As Gerd Theissen points out, in traditions where Satan represents a non-personal force of evil, "nobody need sympathize with him when his resistance is being broken".[44] But in Edwards' scheme Satan is a personal creature whose resistance to goodness never is broken, in the sense that he is never won over to good. God's power defeats him. But God's love is not strong enough to change his refusal to see anything of the divine loveliness: by his steadfast resistance, Satan has "become untouchable for the lure of God's truth and goodness".[45] We feel for Edwards' Satan the ache of rejected love and creaturely fulfillment. We can sympathize too with Satan's Creator. How could such an excellent and beloved creature of God go so horribly wrong? In that creature's eternal hatred of God and fellow creatures, undertones of tragedy and divine vulnerability keep intruding into Edwards' eschatological victory song.

A common interpretation of Edwards' theology locates its center in the omnipotent glory of God. Nowhere is this reading better supported than in Edwards' eschatology. However his treatment of angels and Satan functioned in some ways to provide a counterpoint to his eschatology by echoing another major theological theme: the character of God revealed in Christ. Relying on the best exegetical tradition of his time, Edwards developed a picture of Satan that resisted his "eschatology of glory". It is to Edwards' credit that he refused to exorcise this figure, even though it made his theological performance more complex.

Unlike Jonathan Edwards, Karl Barth lived in an era in which reflection on angels was considered "dispensable and superfluous" to good theological performance. As Barth summed up the dominant view, "The Christian has to do with God alone, with the will and presence of God. What, then, is the point of angels?"[46] Performance expectations had shifted dramatically from Edwards' time, and Barth found many modern theologians "plainly rather peevish and impatient at having to handle the subject" of angels at all:

> And if we are told in Hebrews 13:2 not to be neglectful of hospitality, since some have entertained angels unawares, these theologians are almost anxiously concerned to refuse the angels a lodging in their dogmatics, and think that all things considered they should warn others against extending hospitality to them.[47]

Barth invited angels into his *Church Dogmatics*, because he was convinced that they helped Christian theology address "the problem of heaven on earth", the mystery of the speech and action of the transcendent God in the sphere of human life. Angels deserved imaginative dogmatic treatment because they had "a bearing on our world and our view of the world".[48]

However he found that "a lot of hampering rubbish has accumulated in this field in both ancient and more modern times",[49] requiring him to do much ground clearing before even the right questions could emerge. He pushed aside the ornate, speculative angelologies of the earlier tradition that were enthralled with the existence of angels in their own right, having forgotten that angels "are essentially marginal figures". To return to the musical analogy, Barth saw that angels were ornaments to the major theological themes, not the main melody. In Scripture, Barth insisted "Angels are not independent and autonomous subjects like God and man and Jesus Christ. They cannot, therefore, be made the theme of an independent discussion."[50] The point for Barth at which talk of angels became "really interesting" was the intersection of angelic presence and the economy of grace, where they had a "genuinely necessary function as dynamic factors in that occurrence between God and man".[51]

His depiction of the angelic realm had little in common with the frightening and tumultuous realm of Barth's Europe. Unlike earth, heaven is a morally unambiguous realm where God's will *is* done, where creatures show their "willingness and readiness for helpful participation" in God's "purpose of grace and salvation". "Whatever the manner of heaven", Barth declared confidently, "its being is an obedient being … The presence of God in heaven, the origin and commencement there of His action in the world, makes it necessary that He should find there the obedience of His creature; that His creature in heaven should do His will."[52] Because angels in Barth's scheme were by definition obedient creatures, incapable of falling into enmity with God, they exemplified a creaturely existence immune from the threat of chaos and destruction.

Not only are the angels without sin; they are not even tempted as we are. The angels' obedience is perfect because, unlike human beings, they have no creaturely autonomy. They lack the personal agency and "reciprocal relationships" by which human creatures can belong to themselves as well as to God. In Barth's brave new heaven, angels "have no history or aims or achievements of their own. They have no profile or character, no mind or will of their own. They have all these things, yet not as their own possession, but wholly and exclusively as God is so rich in relation to them. They are themselves only a possession, His possession."[53] This "apparent ontological weakness" of the angels is really their glory. The point of their obedient existence is witness to God's reconciliation of the world in Jesus Christ. Unlike human beings, whose witness to God always partakes of their creaturely particularity, angels are "pure witnesses" who point to God in an "utterly selfless and undemanding and purely subservient" way.[54] The human witness is to imitate his angelic counterpart by being "free only to obey and serve" God, and by letting God's relation to the world "quite naturally and self-evidently take precedent in his life over all other concerns".[55]

From the beginning, the angels enjoy an eschatological perch; they witness to the complete victory of the risen Christ over sin, suffering, and death, rather than to the humility and love of the Suffering Servant on earth. They shed light on human beings' earthly spiritual struggles by showing them to be moot. As heavenly creatures, angels "are in an exemplary and perfect way that which constitutes the essence of all creatures and characterises earthly creatures as their origin and goal".[56] The angels disclose that the eschatological goal God has determined for all creatures is an obedience in which "the possibility of deviation or omission does not arise".[57] Barth's vision of essential creaturehood is reminiscent of the rest Augustine envisions for the saints in heaven—though without Augustine's associations of release from contrary experience:

> our nature, made whole by immortality and incorruption, will have no vices and experience no rebellion from within or without. There will

be no need for reason to govern non-existent evil inclinations. God will hold sway over man, the soul over the body; and the happiness in eternal life and law will make obedience sweet and easy.[58]

For Augustine, the saints' sweet and easy obedience did not deny the reality of ultimate angelic and human resistance to God. Earthly disobedience has tragic consequences. For Barth, the identity between angelic freedom and obedience reveals that "the freedom of the earthly creature, of man", is not "the so-called *liberum arbitrium*, i.e., the freedom to become fools".[59] If human beings play the fool on earth, that does not change God's ultimate "determination of their service". Rather than accompanying us along the ruts and bumps of the earthly drama of redemption, angels point resolutely to the glory of its eschatological conclusion.

Barth's angelology, in my judgment, enhanced some themes in his theology and detracted from others. Construing the angels' ministry as witness to God's salvation underscored the importance of the doctrine of revelation in Barth's theology and gave content to the angels' mediatorial role. His admonition to "remember 'Christ alone' at each and every point" encouraged a fitting restraint in Barth's treatment of angels that he found exemplified in Scripture: "Place is found for them in the Bible where the consummating action of God Himself is not yet or no longer visible to man directly." The angels' obedient witness never overshadows that of the True Witness: in the center of the gospel narratives, the angels' "particular light is outshone like that of a candle in the noonday sun".[60] Barth's treatment of angels was an attractive "annex" to his Christology.

The interaction between Barth's angelology and his anthropology was less harmonious. Barth understood anthropology to be "a consequence and analogy of Christology".[61] But it is not clear how to put together what Barth deduced about human creatures from the humanity of Christ, and what he deduced about humans as creatures from the creaturehood of angels. The paradigmatic humanity of Christ reveals what obedience to God looks like in a creature "tempted as we are", with a particular history, character and mind of his own. By contrast, the angels disclose that the "essence of creaturehood" involves neither personal selfhood nor vulnerability. Barth's angelology only exacerbates the question of what kind of obedience ordinary human beings are freed for by the power of God's grace.

Given his insistence on perfect angelic obedience, Barth was naturally peevish and impatient at having to deal with demons, and most concerned to deny them lodging in his dogmatics. He emphatically rejected the theological tradition that posited demons as fallen angels, deriding it as "one of the bad dreams of the older dogmatics". Nor did he find adequate precedent for this doctrine in Scripture, judging the supporting biblical texts, such as Jude 6 and II Pet. 2:4, to be "so uncertain and obscure that it is inadvisable to allow them to push us in this direction". Throwing down the theological gauntlet, he declared that "literally all the insights which we have gained concerning the being and ministry of angels, and developed at least concerning the character and activity of demons, are necessarily false if this doctrine is correct".[62] Even this was an understatement, for more than Barth's angelology was at stake. The correctness of the doctrine of fallen angels would call into question almost all of the major themes in his theology. If from the beginning some creatures exemplified irremediable resistance to God's will, Barth's anthropology, soteriology, and eschatology would all require major reworking.

Barth chose the daring theological alternative of denying that Satan was a creature at all. In a tongue-in-cheek reference to Bultmann, he asserted that angels and demons are related "as kerygma and myth". Having "no common root" with angelic creatures, demons are a mythological personification of nothingness, "that element of contradiction and opposition which exists on the left hand of God and is thus subject to His world-dominion". Demons "exist only as God affirms Himself and the creature and thus pronounces a necessary No".[63] They inhabit "a sphere of contradiction and opposition which as such can only be overthrown and hasten to destruction".[64] Since demons are not creatures of God, their mode of existence discloses no truth about the eschatological possibilities of human creatures. Their proclamation that they "can intervene between the grace of God and the salvation of the creature, rendering the grace of God weak and ineffective and hampering and retarding the salvation of the creature" is an outrageous lie. Unlike the angels, demons are not "for God and the creature a relevant and serious factor which has to be taken into account".[65] The "supposedly very realistic demonology" of the Christian tradition must be discarded, "not out of any desire for demythologisation, but because [demons] are not worth it".[66]

For Barth, demons were not an embellishment of the dogmatic score; they were more like the rustle of turning pages, or the tuning of instruments between movements of a piece—a regrettable, though unavoidable, distraction from the beauty of the main melody. It would be perverse to find these theological distractions "dreadfully interesting and give them our serious and perhaps systematic attention".[67] There is deep theological wisdom in not letting creaturely sin and evil become the hub of dogmatic reflection. However, the deliberate asymmetry of Barth's treatment of angels and demons required an idiosyncratic reading of Scripture that seems curious alongside his castigations of both early mythologizers and modern demythologizers for not following the biblical witness on angels closely enough. Dogmatic orientation seems to trump scriptural attentiveness at this point. As Gabriel Fackre notes, "we must wonder if Reformed preoccupation with the divine sovereignty and too much talk in Heideggerian idiom of Nothingness combine in Barth's account to obscure another aspect of created—and fallen—transcendence".[68]

Despite the questions it raises about his exegetical consistency, Barth's decision not to give the devil serious dogmatic attention helped him avoid some common eschatological pitfalls. He refused a dualism in which good and evil are presented as simple eschatological alternatives, with human beings placed precariously in the middle, charged with picking a side. Construing God's relations with human creatures in this way would place God "under a law distinct from Himself, the law of repayment, of reciprocal agreement, of reward and punishment".[69] As Marilyn Adams notes, God's eschatological victory over evil in this scenario would be cast "solely in terms of retributive justice: in the next age [God] will make sure that people will get the rewards and punishments they deserve for their performance in this one". Punishment for human creatures who choose the side of the devil is extermination: "God's only recourse is to revert to his strategy in the days of Noah: to destroy the whole thing (except for a righteous remnant) and start over (his promise in the rainbow notwithstanding)!"[70] By contrast, Barth saw that God is not bound by the same logic as the power of evil. God acts "in independent self-determination directed and characterised only by His own choice and love". God's love toward creatures is neither negated by the power of the devil nor constrained by some general law of eschatological deserts.

Barth linked this conviction about divine freedom with exegetical insight into the function of many of the apocalyptic scenarios in Scripture. He construed them more as urgent warnings and encouragements to Christians, than as reliable guides to future eschatological events. In a way that paralleled the use of end-time language by the biblical writers, Barth's demonology functioned to relativize and restrain human judgments of others, and to warn human beings of the urgency of a hospitable response to God's gracious hospitality towards them. He used eschatological language about demonic powers to effect reform in the present. The one who believes Satan's lies places herself under the threat "that [she] will be granted and finally assigned to a life by and in untruth as the portion which [she herself] has chosen, a life which as such can only be a lost life".[71]

The threat is real in the present realm, where devil's "real and constantly successful" charade operates. But since the devil is not an eschatological symbol in Barth's theology, it is not clear how there can ever be "a lost life" in an ultimate sense, how anything can finally "intervene between the grace of God and the salvation of the creature, rendering the grace of God weak and ineffective". Barth's treatment of both the angels and Satan enhances a portrait of God as "the inevitably successful and free determiner of whatever is".[72] The problem with this eschatological portrait, as Edward Farley points out, is that "The dynamics of redemption and the event of Jesus as Christ depict the activity of God as taking place in connection with unpredictable human responses and adamant resistance."[73] The Christ to which Barth's angels witness is the glorious risen Christ, who has already triumphed over the pseudo-creature Satan. Ironically, it was Jonathan Edwards who better heeded Barth's own counsel to "remember 'Christ alone' at each and every point"; in his scheme both the angels and Satan enhanced the figure of "the crucified Savior". In an eschatology of the cross, the tragedy of creaturely resistance to God must be taken more seriously than Barth's portrayal of angels and demons allows.

A Deferent Freedom

"So then, whatever is said concerning the ministry of angels, let us direct it to the end that, having banished all lack of trust, our hope in God may be more firmly established."[74] John Calvin was right: whatever we may wish to say about angels, the point of the exercise is spiritual edification. I will end by noting a virtue that I find particularly nourished by reflections on the angelic realm: deferent freedom.

Angels resist the confines of our usual theological constructions of the relation between God and creatures. They underscore our inability to realize a master narrative of God's creative power and providential care. They complexify the already unsystematic and divergent images of Christian eschatology. They show us the narrowness of the familiar world of our experience. If we resist the temptation to dismiss them entirely, or to force their varied and mysterious presence in Scripture to conform to our dogmatic presuppositions, angels can remind us that our hope in God is more firmly established by heartfelt wonder than by epistemological confidence.

Theologians like me, for whom angels reside in the realm of Paul Ricoeur's "second naivete", can also find spiritual edification in the direction that reflection on angels provides for understanding our relationship to the communion of saints. Much of the Christian tradition's reflection on angels and demons may strike us as flamboyantly speculative, but as H. Richard Niebuhr notes in another context, "we are inclined to regard all beliefs to be speculative which are founded on analyses we have not ourselves made". In reflections on angels we cannot discount the possibility that these traditions rest "not at all upon speculations but upon genuine inquiries" into realities of the life of faith and upon "real communications of God" of which we are unaware. Deference to our fellow believers prevents us from declaring flatly that "that which we do not experience and which we have not been able to experience does not exist".[75] Our theological discomfort with a richly ornamented communal piety need not become a normative aesthetic.

On the other hand, even if the scriptural and theological tradition did exhibit more uniformity in its reflections on the angelic realm, this "cloud of witnesses" would not usurp our theological freedom to follow some of our own intuitions about proper theological performance. Niebuhr captures the dialectic eloquently:

> We shall consider only one reality as normative, God in Christ, Christ in God, to whom the faith of the past and ours is directed and from whom

it proceeds. And in this situation we shall not be afraid to speak of what we know, but neither shall we be without reverence for what other men have known, though we no longer know it or do not yet know it.[76] What is needed in theological reflections on the angelic realm is a deferent freedom, in which we claim the freedom craft our own theological performance in the way that seems best to us, while exhibiting deference to those who delight in ornamenting the main themes of God in Christ. We may even hope that "sometime, perhaps, we shall understand the reality to which they refer".[77]

NOTES

1 Leon Plantinga, private correspondence. I am grateful for the comments and suggestions of Burton Cooper, Susan Garrett, Kathryn Johnson, Kathryn Tanner, and Miroslav Volf.
2 However, there are numerous, conflicting ancient traditions about the creaturely origins of demons, and their "fall" from goodness. Several related theories about demonic origins emerged in early Jewish and Christian reflections on Genesis 6:1–4, which tells of "sons of God" who mated with the "daughters of men", who in turn (according to the conventional reading of the passage) gave birth to the *nephilim* or "giants". In *1 Enoch*, the evil spirits come forth from the slain bodies of the giants and are destined to corrupt affairs on earth "until the great age is consummated". In *Jubilees* and Justin Martyr's *Apology* the spirits are said to be the direct offspring of the angels and women. Some ancient writers assume that not only the offspring-demons but also the fallen angels themselves lead humans astray.
3 Michael Welker, "Angels in the Biblical Traditions: An Impressive Logic and the Imposing Problem of Their Hypercomplex Reality", *Theology Today* 51, no. 3 (October 1994), p. 368.
4 Richard Lewontin, "Billions and Billions of Demons", review of *The Demon-Haunted World: Science as a Candle in the Dark*, by Carl Sagan, in *New York Review of Books*, Jan. 9, 1997. I am indebted to Neal Plantinga for this reference.
5 See, for example, Walter Wink's trilogy, *Naming the Powers, Unmasking the Powers*, and *Engaging the Powers*. The Vatican's recent publication of a revised Catholic rite for exorcism, which reaffirms the existence and work of the Devil, may be seen as a response to widespread belief in spirits in the non-western church.
6 Friedrich Schleiermacher, *The Christian Faith*, H. R. Mackintosh and J. S. Stewart (eds) (Edinburgh: T&T Clark, 1986), p. 156.
7 Ibid., p. 170.
8 Ibid., p. 169.
9 Ibid., p. 167.
10 Quoted in Karl Barth, *Church Dogmatics*, G. W. Bromiley and R. J. Ehrlich (trans.) (Edinburgh: T&T Clark, 1955), III/3, p. 377.
11 Schleiermacher, p. 167.
12 Kathryn Tanner, *Theories of Culture: A New Agenda for Theology* (Minneapolis, MN: Fortress Press, 1997), p. 76.
13 Ibid., p. 70.
14 Schleiermacher, p. 156.
15 Tanner, p. 88.
16 Garrett Green has rightly called attention to the vital role of theological imagination, in which "a subject matter that is not available to direct observation is mediated by selective and integrating images, which are themselves of necessity drawn from our experience of reality that *is* immediately accessible, that is, from the 'mesocosmic' world of present, everyday experience—what can be directly seen, heard, handled, felt." *Imagining God: Theology and the Religious Imagination* (Grand Rapids, MI: Wm. B. Eerdmans Publishing Company, 1989), p. 66. However, I think Green overestimates the determinative power of the biblical paradigm in theological imagination.

17   Gabriel Fackre, "Angels Heard and Demons Seen", *Theology Today* 51, no. 3 (October 1994), p. 348.
18   Barth, p. 371.
19   See Jonathan Edwards, *Religious Affections*, John Smith (ed), in Perry Miller (ed), *The Works of Jonathan Edwards*, vol. 2 (New Haven, CT: Yale University Press, 1959). Edwards' reflections on angels and demons are from the set of lifelong private theological inquiries known as the "Miscellanies". Roughly the first 500 of these entries have been published in *The "Miscellanies," a-500*, Thomas A. Schafer (ed), in Harry S. Stout (ed), *The Works of Jonathan Edwards*, vol. 13 (New Haven, CT: Yale University Press, 1994). I will be drawing on entries written during the 1740s, which are forthcoming in the third volume of the "'Miscellanies" in the Yale series, Amy Plantinga Pauw (ed). Reference will be according to the entry numbers assigned by Edwards.
20   Martha C. Nussbaum, *Love's Knowledge: Essays on Philosophy and Literature* (New York, NY: Oxford University Press, 1990), quoted in Thomas G. Long, "Why Jessica Mitford was Wrong", *Theology Today*, 55, no. 4 (January 1999), p. 508.
21   No. 938.
22   No. 941.
23   Jonathan Edwards, *Ethical Writings*, Paul Ramsey (ed), in John Smith (ed), *The Works of Jonathan Edwards*, vol. 8 (New Haven, CT: Yale University Press, 1989), p. 233.
24   No. 939. Here Edwards was following Hebrews 1:14, "Are not all angels spirits in the divine service, sent to serve for the sake of those who are to inherit salvation?"
25   Ibid.
26   No. 875.
27   No. 937.
28   Dietrich Bonhoeffer, *Letters and Papers from Prison*, enlarged edition, Eberhard Bethge (ed) (New York, NY: MacMillan, 1979), p. 381.
29   Of course, in a theology in which God is portrayed this way, one would expect a similar depiction of angels. For an exposition and critique of this view of God, see Nicholas Wolterstorff, "Suffering Love", in Thomas V. Morris (ed), *Philosophy and the Christian Faith* (Notre Dame, IN: University of Notre Dame Press, 1988).
30   No. 936.
31   *Ethical Writings*, pp. 373–374.
32   Bonhoeffer, *Creation and Fall: A Theological Exposition of Genesis 1–3*, John W. DeGruchy (ed), Douglas Stephen Bax (trans.), in *Dietrich Bonhoeffer Works*, vol. 3 (Minneapolis, MN: Fortress Press, 1997), p. 104.
33   John Milton, *Paradise Lost*, in Mortimer J. Adler (ed), *Great Books of the Western World* (Chicago, IL: Encyclopaedia Britannica, 1952), vol. 29, p. 190. We know from Edwards' catalog of reading that he was familiar with this work.
34   No. 936. See Isa. 14:12.
35   No. 980.
36   No. 936.
37   Ibid.
38   Marilyn McCord Adams, "Separation and Reversal in Luke-Acts", in Thomas V. Morris (ed), *Philosophy and the Christian Faith*, p. 104 (bracketed insertions are mine).
39   Wendy Farley, *Tragic Vision and Divine Compassion: A Contemporary Theodicy* (Louisville, KY: Westminster/John Knox Press, 1990), p. 91. See her keen analysis of Tolkien's portrayal of the power of evil in *The Lord of the Rings*, pp. 89–92.
40   *Ethical Writings*, p. 237.
41   No. 936.
42   Ibid.
43   *Ethical Writings*, pp. 390–391.
44   Gerd Theissen, "The Ambivalence of Power in Early Christianity", in Cynthia L. Rigby (ed), *Power, Powerlessness, and the Divine: New Inquiries in Bible and Theology* (Atlanta, GA: Scholars Press, 1997), p. 28.
45   Miroslav Volf, *Exclusion and Embrace: A Theological Exploration of Identity, Otherness and Reconciliation* (Nashville, TN: Abingdon Press, 1996), p. 297. Volf is writing about the tragic recalcitrance of some human sinners. But his words apply to Edwards' portrait of Satan as well: "Can we assume that the violent will want to be transformed so as to want the

well-being of the other? Underlying the theology of judgment in the Apocalypse is the assumption that nothing is potent enough to change those who insist on remaining beasts and false prophets."

46 Barth, *Church Dogmatics*, G. W. Bromiley (trans.) (Edinburgh: T&T Clark, 1961), III/3, p. 415.
47 Ibid., p. 415.
48 Ibid., p. 411.
49 Ibid., p. xi.
50 Ibid., p. 371.
51 Ibid., p. 387.
52 Ibid., pp. 516, 444.
53 Ibid., p. 480.
54 Ibid., p. 484.
55 Karl Barth, *Church Dogmatics*, G. W. Bromiley (trans.) (Edinburgh: T&T Clark, 1961), IV/3, pp. 599, 602.
56 Barth, III/3, p. 480.
57 Ibid., p. 493.
58 Augustine, *City of God*, Vernon J. Bourke (ed) (Garden City, NY: Image Books, 1958), p. 481.
59 Barth, III/3, p. 531.
60 Ibid., p. 502.
61 Ibid., p. 500.
62 Ibid., p. 531.
63 Ibid., pp. 519, 523.
64 Ibid., p. 522.
65 Ibid., p. 525.
66 Ibid., p. xii.
67 Ibid., p. 519.
68 Fackre, p. 348.
69 Barth, IV/3, p. 460.
70 Adams, p. 94.
71 Barth, IV/3, p. 462.
72 *Divine Empathy: A Theology of God* (Minneapolis, MN: Fortress Press, 1996), p. 305, note 1.
73 Ibid., p. 310.
74 John Calvin, *Institutes of the Christian Religion*, John T. McNeill (ed) Library of Christian Classics (Philadelphia, PA: Westminster Press, 1960), vol. 1, p. 171 (I.xiv.12).
75 H. Richard Niebuhr, *Faith on Earth: An Inquiry into the Structure of Human Faith*, Richard R. Niebuhr (ed) (New Haven, CT: Yale University Press, 1989), pp. 106–107. Niebuhr is discussing the personhood of the Holy Spirit.
76 Ibid., p. 108.
77 Ibid., p. 108.

CHAPTER 4

THE ESCHATOLOGICAL BODY: GENDER, TRANSFORMATION, AND GOD

SARAH COAKLEY

I. Introduction: Bodily Obsessions

In this essay I shall attempt to substantiate what may appear to be an initially implausible thesis. I shall be arguing that the obsessive interest in the "body" which has been such a marked feature of late twentieth-century Western culture hides a profound eschatological longing; only a *theological* vision of a particular sort, I shall suggest, can satisfy it. More specifically, I shall test this contention by reference to the work of one leading post-modern secular feminist, Judith Butler, whose work on gender,[1] and the sub-version of "gender binaries", is fast achieving the status of dogma in some American women's studies and religious studies circles. Butler, perhaps, we may see as the high-priestess of anti-essentialist feminism, presiding (by means of suitably liturgical *performative* utterance) over the sacrificial death of gender stability. Yet Butler's ingenious attempts to escape the repressive net of sexual stereotypes are—I shall suggest—ironic, if ultimately depressing, secularized counterparts of an *ascetical* programme of gender fluidity into the divine that Christian tradition may hold out to us, especially as we find it in the work of the fourth-century Gregory of Nyssa; and Nyssa's pro-gramme works with a necessarily eschatological *telos*. This unlikely pair of interlocutors, then, will form the focus of my analysis: in introducing Judith Butler to Gregory of Nyssa, I shall not merely be inviting a comparison of a post-modern perspective on "body" and "self" with a pre-modern one (such comparisons have all the dangers of anachronism, but can nonetheless prove theologically instructive[2]); rather, my goal is to educe a theological answer to a latent—if repressed—eschatological question in our millennial cultural milieu.

Sarah Coakley
The Divinity School, Harvard University, 45 Francis Avenue, Cambridge, MA 02138, USA

But first we need to ask: why do "bodies" "matter" so much? No one can have failed to notice the obsession with the "body" that has gripped the late-twentieth-century popular imagination; yet this very phenomenon bears all the marks of our current deepest *aporias*, fears and longings.[3] The notable explosion of thought and literature on the subject of the "body" in recent decades[4] has, for a start, begged a question of definition which is not so easily grasped, let alone answered. It is as if we are clear about an agreed cultural obsession, but far from assured about its referent. As Judith Butler herself has put it, "I tried to discipline myself to stay on the subject, but found I could not fix bodies as objects of thought ... Inevitably, I began to consider that this resistance was essential to the matter in hand."[5] Or, as put from a rather different methodological perspective, by Mary Douglas: "Just as it is true that everything symbolizes the body, so it is equally true that the body symbolizes *everything else*."[6] It seems that "bodies" are as elusive as they are ubiquitous—curiously hard to get our "hands" around, even as we constantly refer to them as the locus of potential meaning.

The question that seems to press in a post-modern age is this: if we[7] can no longer count on any universal "grand narrative" to bear the burden of religious and philosophical needs for meaning-making, is it perhaps only resistant fleshliness that we can look to as an Archimedean point of stability—a seemingly unambiguous focus for longings, myths and quasi-religious hopes? Yet on closer reflection this too—the post-modern "body"—becomes subject to infinitely variable social constructions. The "body" thus comes to bear huge, and paradoxical, pressure in post-modern thought: just as its Enlightenment partner, the "mind/soul" of Cartesianism, is seen off with almost unexamined vehemence,[8] so, simultaneously, what is left (the "body") becomes infinitely problematized and elusive. It is all that we have, but we seemingly cannot grasp it; nor, more frighteningly, are we sure that we can control the political forces that seek to regiment it. Devoid now of religious meaning or of the capacity for any fluidity into the divine, shorn of any expectation of new life beyond the grave, it has shrunk to the limits of individual fleshliness; hence our only hope seems to reside in keeping it alive, youthful, consuming, sexually active, and jogging on (literally), for as long as possible.

Yet even as we do this (in America, at any rate, with an unexamined neo-ascetical self-righteousness, what from a Christian standpoint we may deem a *sweaty* Pelagianism), the anxious question presses: what is this "body" that I "have"? From what other site of control am "I" pummeling it into submission, beauty or longevity? Herein lie what Daniel Bell has, in another context, called our "cultural contradictions".[9] For in the late twentieth-century affluent West, the "body", to be sure, is sexually affirmed, but also puritanically punished in matters of diet or exercise; continuously stuffed with consumerist goods, but guiltily denied particular foods in aid of the "salvation" of a longer life; taught that there is nothing *but* it (the "body"), and yet asked to discipline it with an "I" that still refuses complete materialistic reduction.

Despite the legion cries for *greater* "embodiment", for a notion of self as body,[10] the spectres of religious and philosophical dualism die hard;[11] somewhere the last smile on a Cartesian Cheshire cat still lurks, or is it even a more ancient manifestation of "soul"?

It is, I suggest, precisely these contradictions that should alert us to a latent cultural yearning in the matter of "bodies"—not towards the immediate sexual fulfillment that appears as the ubiquitous cultural palliative (if only in fantasy), but an equally erotic yearning towards a more elusive eschatological goal. From this perspective the bodily obsessions just described—the quest for longevity, beauty, health, sexual performance—bespeak a prevailing denial of death.[12] But as Caroline Bynum remarks, in a penetrating little essay entitled "Why All the Fuss about the Body? A Medievalist's Perspective",[13] it is also in contemporary "popular" cultural products, such as the film *Truly, Madly, Deeply*, that we encounter an incipient countervailing *acknowledgment* of the facts of death, of a longing for a body beyond death, and of confusion in the face of the changed features of the ghostly body (which, interestingly, will not return without bringing a host of other new "dead" friends with it; the body beyond death, it seems, is intrinsically communal, much to the disgust of the grieving widow in this entrancing and evocative film).

Is, then, the post-modern *intellectual* obsession with "body" as it relates to the theorizing of sexuality and gender an equally subtle subterfuge, another evasive ploy? Is it perhaps fuelling, as well as feeding off, more "popular" manifestations of death-denial, and screening us from political and social horrors that we otherwise cannot face? That, at any rate, is the view of Terry Eagleton, in his pounding assault on the *Illusions of Postmodernism*;[14] and it is a thesis not without point. For Eagleton shows how post-modern loss of faith in "teleology" (what Eagleton terms "holophobia") has undermined the political commitment to classic socialist goals and diverted us from the grinding poverty of the world's dispossessed; yet meanwhile the "power of capital" (a new "grand narrative" if ever there was one) has sneaked up and taken us over whilst we have been comforting ourselves with the more sensuous and narcissistic "new somatics": "The body ... is currently en route to becoming the greatest fetish of all", Eagleton charges, and in this he tars "feminism" undifferentiatedly with the same brush, for he sees much of it as all-too-comfortably compatible with the new global capitalism.[15] Bynum's contention is not dissimilar. For her, "modern treatments of person and body have recently concentrated rather too much on issues of gender and sexuality to the detriment of our awareness of other things" (and here she enumerates death, work, and—elsewhere—"fecundity").[16]

But it is here that I shall beg to differ from Bynum's (and Eagleton's) otherwise perceptive and illuminating analyses. By focusing on the feminist theory of Judith Butler, I shall attempt to demonstrate that her radical theory of gender "performativity" leads us inexorably to the questions of eschatological longing that Bynum seeks to retrieve, and thereby—albeit unintentionally—to the horizon of a *divine* "grand narrative". Whilst Butler's own prescriptions relate only to a secular realm and are tinged with a deep pessimism about radical social change, her thematizations of desire, of gender fluidity, and of subversive personal agency all echo older, theistically-oriented traditions of personal transformation within and beyond the "body" of this mortal life. Butler has been accused of "dissolving" the body into "discourse"; I shall argue, on the contrary (and doubtless to Butler's own dismay!), that her theory has the remaining marks of a body longing for transformation into the divine. Like Gregory of Nyssa, with whom I shall compare her, Butler sees the point of "practices" of transformation that start now but have their final goal in the future: they create the future by enacting its possibilities. As Jürgen Moltmann has well said of a falsely-futuristic eschatology, "The person who presses forward to the end of life *misses life itself.*[17] Both Judith Butler and Gregory of Nyssa, as I shall now attempt to demonstrate, know the meaning of that aphorism and present us with visions of bodily (and gendered) transformations that press forward from the present.

II. Judith Butler on Gender Performativity

Butler's impenetrably opaque prose obfuscates as much as it reveals: this is arguably all part of her strategy of linguistic subversion. (It is certainly a challenge to the analytically-trained mind.[18]) At once speculative theorist and practical reformer, Butler invites her reader into a dizzying engagement with (strangely masculinist) forebears as diverse as Nietzsche, Freud, Althusser, Austin, Foucault and Kripke. Not all of these are invoked immediately in her earliest work; but previous feminist theorists of whom she is critical from the start include de Beauvoir, Irigaray, Kristeva and Wittig—all figures whom she regards as veering too closely to gender essentialism. Out of this strange concoction of heroes, detractors and resources, she constructs in *Gender Trouble* (1990) her central theory about the persistent oppressiveness of compulsory heterosexuality. "Gender" is not "natural" but repetitively "performed": "The univocity of sex, the internal coherence of gender, and the binary framework for both sex and gender are ... regulatory fictions that consolidate and naturalize the convergent power regimes of masculine and heterosexist oppression."[19] Thus the "body" is no "ready surface awaiting signification, but ... a set of boundaries, individual and social, politically signified and maintained".[20] Sex is "[n]o longer believable as an interior 'truth' of dispositions and identity", but is rather a "performatively enacted signification ..., one that, released from its naturalized interiority and surface, can occasion the parodic proliferation and subversive play of gendered meanings."[21] Hence Butler, as a lesbian theorist, is out to make "gender trouble", "not through the strategies that figure a *utopian* beyond, but through the mobilization, subversive confusion, and proliferation of precisely those constitutive categories that seek to keep gender in its place by posturing as the foundational illusions of identity".[22]

Butler's theory, we note, assumes both a fluidity of gender and its (re)creation through repeated practice. There is nothing "natural" about it; indeed "de-naturalization" of gender is the point of the whole project.[23] But this is not to say (as Butler is often misunderstood) that gender can be constituted at will, or by mere verbal fiat; that would be to underestimate the "established" nature of the gender binaries that Butler seeks to de-stabilize: "To enter into the repetitive practices of this terrain is not a choice, for the 'I' that might enter is always already inside: there is no possibility of agency or reality outside of the discursive practices that give those terms the intelligibility that they have."[24] Thus: "The task is not whether to repeat, but how to repeat or, indeed, to repeat and, through a radical proliferation of gender, *to displace* the very gender norms that enable the repetition itself."[25] The "performance" of gender is, on this view, *both* a repeated (if unconscious) act in favour of "compulsory heterosexuality" *and* a potentially subversive act of homosexual or lesbian defiance; but the former undeniably has the cultural upper-hand, and provides the resistant backcloth to the latter. Nonetheless, to some undisclosed extent we can at least spoof the social forces of gender that so exercise us.

The spiritual significance of Butler's analysis should at this point give us pause. The "denaturalization" of sex and gender is, as we shall shortly see, a theme shared with an older tradition of ascetical transformation. The possibilities for labile, fluid transformation towards a goal of liberation and personal authenticity is what Butler's vision has in common with this more ancient wisdom. Moreover, it is the yoking of "practice" (Butler's "performance") and theory that also strikes a note of spiritual reminiscence: change cannot occur by mere thought, but is precisely the product of arduous exercise —an exercise *against* the grain of the predominant cultural assumption, the assumption, that is, of heterosexual "marriage and giving in marriage". To the extent that this vision of transformation hangs over Butler's theorizing, then, it begs a question about the possibilities of "grace"; whereas a more cynical reading would suggest that Butler's theory of resistance is merely reinstantiating the conditions of sexual oppression against which she chafes.

Martha Nussbaum, in an intemperate recent review of Butler's corpus,[26] takes the latter interpretative perspective. If "performing" resistance represents the heart of Butler's thesis, she argues, then does it not signal the *necessity* of the remaining conditions of sexual oppression? "For Butler", she charges, "the act of subversion is so riveting, so sexy, that it is a bad dream to think that the world will actually get better. What a bore equality is! No bondage, no delight. In this way [Butler's] pessimistic erotic anthropology offers support to an amoral anarchistic politics."[27] Such a critique has its point (since Butler does not explicitly promise us that the world will ever become less "compulsorily heterosexist"); but it fails to engage with the profounder levels of spiritual yearning that I detect in Butler's text.

In other ways, too, Butler's theory of "body" is capable of serious distortion. Bynum is not the only one to charge her with dissolving bodily matter into "discourse". (Were this so, it would be an ironic triumph for feminism, so to elevate the final power of the "word" over body.) But Butler's second major book on gender theory, *Bodies that Matter* (1993), explicitly addresses this question, and wards off the suggestion of the reduction of physical bodiliness to mere forms of verbal instantiation. "Performance", to be sure, as becomes clearer in Butler's new usage here of Austin's *How to Do Things with Words* (1962), effects what it proclaims verbally. But it is gender that is performed, not the material bodies themselves. Language cannot *create* bodies (that would be an odd claim indeed); rather, Butler is insisting that there is no access to bodies that is not already a gendered access: "there is no reference to a pure body which is not at the same time a further formation of that body … In philosophical terms, the constative claim is always to some degree performative."[28] Here we see clearly, then, the distinction in Butler between bodiliness and subjectivity; the one cannot simply be reduced to the other. As one perceptive commentator (Amy Hollywood) has put it, "Butler's most important work in *Bodies That Matter* … lies in its assertion that sites of resistance to dominant discourses can be articulated without relying on a concept of materiality that lies untouched by that discourse. Rather than arguing for a transcending idealism of a transcendent materiality, Butler demonstrates the … possibilities for transcendence that emerge in and through complex bodily experiences."[29] It is the nature of that "transcendence" with which we are especially concerned—an excess of possibility that refuses to limit "desire" to its physical locus of pleasure. "Desire" for Butler always signals a form of "loss", an obscured yearning, an exclusion of possibilities that "compulsory heterosexuality" rules out. Again, we shall have reason to compare this with a more explicitly Christian perception of unending desire (for God) that informs Gregory's "erotic" spirituality.

In Butler's more recent work, it is a post-Foucaultian analysis of "power" that comes to the fore in her analysis, and at points suggests comparison with the "Yahweh" of her Jewish heritage who still lurks at the corners of her discussion.[30] "Power", as one critic has acutely noted, is now the "God-term" in Butler's text; no wonder, then, that this "power" is inescapable, the only modality in and through which "agency" even becomes possible: "there is no formation of the subject without a passionate attachment to subjection".[31] Yet out of this learned subjection, even out of degradation, come the possibilities of hope and resistance. (Somewhere the myth of cross and resurrection lurks, mediated no doubt through the Hegel who forms the focus of Butler's meditations in *The Psychic Life of Power*.) Less clear now than before is the *optimistic* call to fluid gendered transformation; more clear is her insistence that speech can effect occasional punctures in existing power relations.[32]

Why does Butler's vision exercise such "power" itself? Despite Nussbaum's derisive critique of Butler's "hip defeatism", Butler's work continues to exercise an uncanny degree of influence. Somehow it is the allure of gender liberation (not now sexual liberation, note) that fascinates the late-twentieth-century mind, the prospect of an escape from stereotype, the hope of an elusive personal transformation beyond normal human expectations and restrictions. But to what (eschatological) end? That is a question not answered by Butler herself, although surely her argument begs it. The comparison with an equally fluid Christian spirituality of gender now becomes pressing.

III. Gregory of Nyssa (c. 330–c. 395) and the Transformations of Gender

Nyssa is, as in many other matters, notoriously inconsistent in his theorizing about the resurrection body and our own eschatological end;[33] sure it is, however, that his fascinating suggestions in this area should not be considered in abstraction from his equally subtle understandings of gender, which are deeply entangled with them. Bynum, in her recent magisterial volume *The Resurrection of the Body* (1995) gives an illuminating account of Gregory's eschatology but says relatively little about the place of gender in it. We are indebted to Verna Harrison for a first careful consideration of Nyssa's theory of gender, and I draw most gratefully on her pioneering work.[34] However there are points in Nyssa's consideration of gender stereotype (what Butler would call the oppressive "gender binaries") which need deeper consideration than I think has yet been given: Gregory's gender theory, like Butler's, does not claim to *obliterate* the binaries that remain culturally normative, but seeks —also like Butler—to find a transformative way through them. Whereas in Butler, however, this escape is effected by punctiliar subversive acts of "performativity", in Gregory it represents a life-long ascetical programme, a purification and redirection of *eros* towards the divine, a final withdrawal from the whirligig of marriage, child-rearing, the quest for social status and financial security.[35] In Gregory's case this is especially poignant, since we know that he was married as a younger man and he writes of the tragic death of children with enormous insight and grief; but nowhere—and how interestingly contrastive is this with Augustine—does he agonize with guilt or fear about the sexual act itself. Indeed, one might argue on the contrary that his spirituality of progressive ascent and increasing loss of noetic control (as set out in *The Life of Moses*) is figured precisely by analogy with the procreative act; Gregory says as much in the introduction to his *Commentary on the Song of Songs*—that the passage from the physical to the spiritual is not effected by repression of the memory of physical love: "I hope that my commentary will be a guide for the more fleshly-minded, since the wisdom hidden [in the Song of Songs] *leads* to a spiritual state of the soul."[36]

As Bynum shows with exemplary clarity, Gregory's eschatological body is an ever-changing one; like Origen, the Syriac writers Ephrem and Aphrahat, and Cyril of Jerusalem before him, he takes Paul's "seed" metaphor in 1 Cor. 15 to heart: the body is labile and changing in this life and is on its way to continuing change into incorruptibility in the next. (This is *unlike* a rival tradition forged in reaction to Origen, which sees the resurrection body as the reassemblage of "bits", or as what Bynum finds in Augustine as a final freezing of "flux".[37]) For Gregory, however, change does not necessarily signal decay, but can on the contrary mark the endless transformations "from glory to glory". Famously re-defining "perfection" as "never arriving"— a daring move for a Platonist—he similarly understands the partaking of Eucharist in this life as an already-anticipated reception of heavenly food. We are on a continuum, then, from this "body" to our "angelic" future "bodies", and death need not be a *dramatic* shift in the case of a holy ascetical body, as we shall see.

Where, then, does gender fit into this picture? As is well known, and Verna Harrison has explicated with especial care, Gregory holds (on the basis of a particular reading of Gen. 1:27, in conjunction with Gal. 3:28) that the original creation was of non-sexed (that is, non-genitalized) beings; his text *On the Making of Man* suggests that it was only *en route*, so to speak, to the Fall, that "man" was distinguished from "woman".[38] So too, at the end of times, as he expounds in *On Those who have Fallen Asleep*, we shall expect to be de-genitalized again, and so receive that angelic status that was our lot originally (the contrast with the Augustine of *The City of God* is of course instructive: Augustine becomes sure that we shall be able to recognise each other as men and women in heaven).[39] It is a mistake, however, as Harrison helps illuminate, to read Gregory here as divorcing our development from the exigencies of *gender*; even if our genitalia are finally irrelevant to our "bodily" condition before God, that does not mean that we are released from what Butler would (rather differently) term the "performances" of gender. On the contrary, the whole point of a life of virginity (as Gregory argues in his early work *De Virginitate*, bemusingly enough written at a time when he was probably married), is to become spiritually "fecund".[40] And the continual purgative transformations of the ascetical life involve forms of gender fluidity and reversal (as we shall show) that undercut and subvert what could be expected of someone living according to the late-antique norms of married gender roles.

Three themes in Gregory's eschatologically-oriented theory of gender strike us now as suggestive points of comparison with Butler's more pessimistic secular alternative. First, we must not overlook (as it is tempting to do) the undeniable examples of Gregory's rehearsal of "gender binaries". A particularly revealing example of this phenomenon occurs at the beginning of Book II of *The Life of Moses* (1–8).[41] There Gregory discusses the exegetical meaning to be attached to the fact that "Moses was born at the time Pharaoh issued the decree for *male* offspring to be destroyed": how are we now to "imitate" this, he asks? Surely coming to birth (as a "male") is not something in our power to imitate? However Gregory immediately rehearses here *both* a binary gender stereotype *and* an insistence that gender is fluid and volitional: "For the material and passionate disposition to which human nature is carried when it falls is the female form of life ... The austerity and intensity of virtue is the male birth ... (2). [But] ... In mutable nature nothing can be observed which is always the same ... We are in some manner our own parents [literally, "fathers"], giving birth to ourselves by our own free choice in accordance with whatever we wish to be, whether male or female, moulding ourselves to the teaching of virtue or vice" (3). Is then the stereotype of "female" passion or vice left intact by Gregory? It is a nice point, just as it is a nice point whether Butler's subversive "performativity" of gender needs the gender binaries it seeks to upend. But Gregory adds a further complexification—not found in Butler—when he earlier suggests that such disjunctive gender binaries apply as points of reference primarily for "those who wander outside virtue" (Book I, 11), that is, for mere beginners on the slope of Moses's mystical ascent. Abraham and Sarah (12) are set before such as exemplars, "the men to Abraham and the women to Sarah"; but then, of course, it turns out that they do not represent the "virtue=male" and "passion=female" binary previously named; indeed, with their example we are already well on the way to a set of reversals of such expectation.

Herein lies what I have termed the "eschatologically-oriented" feature of Gregory's complex theory of personal (and gendered) transformation into the divine life, and thus herein too lies our second revealing point of comparison with Butler. As Harrison has tellingly expounded, it is not that either "body" or gender are disposed of in this progressive transformation to a neo-angelic status. Rather, as advances are made in the stages of virtue and contemplation, *eros* finds its truer meaning in God, and gender switches and reversals attend the stages of ascent: the increasingly close relation to Christ marks, in the *Commentary on the Song of Songs*, a shift from active courting of Christ as "Sophia" to passive reception of embraces of Christ as the bridegroom.[42] Does this not, then, at some deeper level merely reinscribe normative gender binaries? This is by no means clear. At this (higher) stage of ascent, one can no longer assume—Jungian importations are distractions here—that the woman ascetic is "primarily" enacting the pole of gender associated at the outset with the "female" and then "adding" "male" virtues to the amalgam. On the contrary, the fascinating banter between Gregory and his older sister Macrina in *On the Soul and the Resurrection* give the lie to such a suggestion. Here, as in the related *Life of Macrina*, Gregory takes the part of the passions and Macrina manifests the stern rational asceticism in which Gregory manifestly fails.[43] As Rowan Williams has put it in a deft analysis of this interaction, its implications for "soul", "body" and gender are subtle ones: "For Gregory ... we could say, there is no such *thing* as the soul in itself; it is always implicated in contingent matter, and even its final liberation for pilgrimage into God ... depends ... upon the deployment and integration of bodiliness and animality ... the ungenderedness of the soul is never the actual state of a real subject."[44] Part, at least, of this could be applauded by Butler too, we could now suggest. But what she cannot assert unambiguously is that divine referent that forms the final point of meaning in Gregory, what Williams thematizes as "that fundamental *eros* for the endless God that binds the polyphony of our intentionality into some sort of unity".[45]

Our third instructive point of comparison with Butler leads on from here. Butler speaks little of death; yet death, as Gregory well sees, is the most incisive test of a person's life. (Or, as Stanley Hauerwas has put it recently, "Perfection is the art of dying",[46] an aphorism that fits interestingly in Gregory's case with his assurance that "Perfection is never arriving".) As we have already hinted, death for Gregory is merely a passage into further "bodily" —albeit de-genitalized—life; for his sister Macrina, already so holy that she becomes a "relic" anticipatorily on her death-bed, the continuum between this life and the next is almost complete. Even the little scar on her breast from a miraculous earlier cure of cancer remains, however; as with Christ's scarred risen body, nothing is lost that represents suffering confronted and overcome: "a memorial of the divine intervention, the result and the occasion of perpetual turning toward God through the action of grace".[47] Bynum writes of this touching passage that it is really always Macrina that Gregory has in mind when he tries to speak of the eschatological body: "The resurrected body is both the ascetic who becomes a relic while still alive and the relic that continues after death the changelessness acquired through asceticism."[48] Do we not perhaps detect a yearning for such completion in Butler's remorselessly sophisticated and tortured maneuvers?

IV. Conclusions: Gender, Transformation and God

I have been suggesting in this essay that Judith Butler's profound desire to shift or subvert the weight of "gender binaries" does not grip our late-twentieth-century imaginations for no reason. Much is at stake here; and it is more—frankly—than a debate about politics, speech and homophobia, important though that is. Rather what seems to be being enacted is the gesturing to an eschatological horizon which will give mortal flesh final significance, a horizon in which the restless, fluid post-modern "body" can find some sense of completion without losing its mystery, without succumbing again to "appropriate" or restrictive gender roles. In introducing Judith Butler to Gregory of Nyssa I have courted the dangerous charge of anachronism for the sake of a spiritual challenge of some severity: for it is not, note, the goal of Gregory's vision to enjoy various forms of previously-banned sexual pleasure; or to escape or sneer at a supposedly "repressive" pornography law. Rather, *Gregory's* vision of final "erotic" fulfillment demands an asceticism costing not less than everything; and to a culture fed on bowdlerized Freud and equally bowdlerized Foucault[49]—in which erotic "purification" can seemingly only signal "repression"—this is hardly likely to have instant appeal. That Gregory's insights may nonetheless provide us with the clues to some of our profoundest cultural riddles about the "body" it has nonetheless been the burden of this paper to suggest; odd, is it not (or not so odd?), that we needed the anguished insights of a secularized Jewish lesbian feminist to remind us of this deep strand of longing and wisdom.[50]

NOTES

1 Butler's four influential books on gender to date are: *Gender Trouble: Feminism and the Subversion of Identity* (New York, NY: Routledge, 1990); *Bodies that Matter: On the Discursive Limits of "Sex"* (New York, NY: Routledge, 1993); *The Psychic Life of Power: Theories in Subjection* (Stanford, CA: Stanford University Press, 1997); and *Excitable Speech: A Politics of the Performative* (New York, NY: Routledge, 1997).

2 Caroline Bynum warns against the dangers of such anachronistic comparisons in her article "Why All the Fuss about the Body? A Medievalist's Perspective", in *Critical Inquiry* 22, 1995, pp. 1–33; see pp. 29–30 for Bynum's remarks about Origen and Judith Butler. I wish to acknowledge my indebtedness to Bynum for her inspiration and friendship; in this matter, however, I have chosen to risk her opprobrium for nonetheless comparing two authors from such widely differing contexts.

3 I repeat here some of the material discussed in the introduction to my edited volume, *Religion and the Body* (Cambridge: Cambridge University Press, 1996), pp. 1–12.

4 Extensive bibliographies of this inter-disciplinary literature can be found in (e.g.), M. Feher (with R. Naddaff and N. Tazi), *Fragments for a History of the Body* (New York, NY: Zone Books, 1989); M. McGuire, "Religion and the Body: Rematerializing the Human Body in the Social Sciences of Religion", *Journal of the Scientific Study of Religion* 29, 1990, pp. 283–296; T. J. Csordas, "Embodiment as a Paradigm for Anthropology", *Ethos* 18, 1990, pp. 5–47; and ed. S. Coakley, *Religion and the Body* (see n. 3).

5 J. Butler, *Bodies that Matter*, p. ix.

6 M. Douglas, *Purity and Danger: An Analysis of Concepts of Pollution and Taboo* (London: Routledge & Kegan Paul, 1966), p. 122, my emphasis.

7 I use "we" here, in these next two paragraphs, in a general (secularized) cultural sense.

8 In my article "Visions of the Self in Late Medieval Christianity", in ed. M. McGhee, *Philosophy, Religion and the Spiritual Life* (Cambridge: Cambridge University Press, 1992), pp. 89–103, I have tried to analyse the political and theological reasons for this unexpected vehemence towards the Cartesian heritage.

9 See D. Bell, *The Cultural Contradictions of Capitalism* (New York: Basic Books, 1976).

10 See, *inter alia*, Csordas (n. 4), for a discussion of the need for a more "embodied" vision of the self in anthropology, an account that draws on the philosophy of Merleau-Ponty and the anthropology of Bourdieu.

11 This "cultural contradiction" is well addressed in S. Bordo, *Unbearable Weight: Feminism, Western Culture and the Body* (Berkeley, CA: University of California Press, 1993).

12 For a now-classic account of this phenomenon, see E. Becker, *The Denial of Death* (New York, NY: Free Press, 1973).

13 See n. 2. The discussion of *Truly, Madly, Deeply* is on pp. 10–12.

14 T. Eagleton, *The Illusions of Postmodernism* (Oxford: Blackwell Publishers, 1996).

15 Ibid., p. 25.

16 Bynum, "Why all the Fuss" (see n. 2), p. 33. Also see her *Holy Feast and Holy Fast: The Religious Significance of Food to Medieval Women* (Berkeley, CA: University of California Press, 1987) for an extended exploration of the theme of repressed "fecundity".

17 J. Moltmann, *The Coming of God: Christian Eschatology* (London: SCM Press, 1996), p. xi, my emphasis.

18 Butler has recently won first prize in the annual "Bad Writing Contest" sponsored by the journal *Philosophy and Literature*; the equivalent "honour" in the UK might be appearing in "Pseuds' Corner" in *Private Eye*.

19   *Gender Trouble*, p. 33.
20   Ibid.
21   Ibid.
22   Ibid., p. 34, my emphasis.
23   See ibid., pp. 147–149.
24   Ibid., p. 148.
25   Ibid.
26   Martha C. Nussbaum, "The Professor of Parody", *The New Republic*, February 22, 1999, pp. 37–45.
27   Ibid., p. 44.
28   *Bodies that Matter*, pp. 10–11.
29   Amy Hollywood, "Transcending Bodies", *Religious Studies Review* 25, 1999, p. 14.
30   See, for instance, the discussion of Freud, Žižek and the "unnameable Yahweh" in "Arguing with the Real", *Bodies that Matter*, ch. 7, esp. p. 200. The exploration of Hegel's master/slave parable in *The Psychic Life of Power*, ch. 1, also cannot help but resummon, if only veiledly, the question of divine power.
31   See the illuminating analysis of Butler's recent work by Michael Levenson, "The Performances of Judith Butler", in *Lingua Franca*, 8, September 1998, pp. 61–67, cf. p. 62.
32   Levenson (see n. 31) sees a disjunction here between Butler's two most recent books, *The Psychic Life of Power* and *Excitable Speech* (see n. 1): the former seems less optimistic than her earlier works about opportunities for genuine change in gender expectations; the latter, however, rehearses again the political possibilities for performative utterance.
33   See the classic article by Jean Daniélou, "La Résurrection des Morts chez Grégoire de Nysse", *Vigiliae Christianae* 7, 1953, pp. 154–170. Bynum re-surveys this material in her *The Resurrection of the Body in Western Christianity, 200–1336* (New York, NY: Columbia University Press, 1995), pp. 81–86. A more nuanced account of the changes in Gregory's views on the nature of the resurrected body over the course of his career, and his eventual careful distancing of himself from Origenism, is provided in Morwenna Ludlow, *Universal Salvation: Eschatology through the Eyes of Gregory of Nyssa and Karl Rahner* (Oxford, forthcoming), ch. 2. I am grateful to Morwenna Ludlow for letting me see her MS in preparation.
34   See Verna Harrison, "Male and Female in Cappadocian Theology", *Journal of Theological Studies* 41, 1990, pp. 441–471; and *eadem*, "Gender, Generation and Virginity", *Journal of Theological Studies* 47, 1996, pp. 38–68.
35   This theme is illuminatingly discussed in relation to the Cappadocians in Peter Brown, *The Body and Society: Men, Women, and Sexual Renunciation in Early Christianity* (New York, NY: Columbia University Press, 1988), ch. 14. Mark D. Hart's "Reconciliation of Body and Soul: Gregory of Nyssa's Deeper Theology of Marriage", *Theological Studies* 51, 1990, pp. 450–478, however, gives a brilliant new reading of Gregory's *de Virginitate* (utilizing the interpretative tool of irony), and argues that Gregory saw marriage, as well as celibacy, as a potential school of "non-attachment".
36   Gregory of Nyssa, *Commentary on the Song of Songs*, trans. Casimir McCambley (Brookline, MA: Hellenic College Press, 1987), p. 35 (my emphasis). For the Greek text, see ed. Werner Jaeger, *Gregorii Nysseni Opera* (Leiden: E. J. Brill, 1960–), (hereafter *GNO*), VI, 4.
37   See the discussion in Bynum, *The Resurrection of the Body*, p. 102.
38   See *De opificio hominis*, 16–17, discussed by Harrison (n. 34) in *Journal of Theological Studies* 41, 1990, p. 468.
39   See the discussion of *On Those who have Fallen Asleep* in ibid., p. 469. (For the Greek, see *GNO* IX, 28–68, esp. 63). A comparison with Augustine, *The City of God* XXII, ch. 17, is instructive.
40   See Harrison, *Journal of Theological Studies* 41, 1990, p. 469, citing Gregory's *De Virginitate* (*GNO* VIII, 1, p. 305).
41   In what follows, I am using the CWS translation, *The Life of Moses*, trans. A. H. Malherbe and E. Ferguson (New York, NY: Paulist Press, 1978), see pp. 55–57 (Bk. II), and pp. 31–32 (Bk. I). For the Greek, see *GNO* VII, 1, 34–37 and 4–6 respectively.
42   See Verna Harrison's exposition of this material from the *First Homily on the Song of Songs* in *Journal of Theological Studies* 47, 1996, pp. 58–62. For the Greek of the first homily, see *GNO* VI, 14–42.
43   See *On the Soul and the Resurrection*, trans. Catherine P. Roth (Crestwood, NY: Saint Vladimir's Seminary Press, 1993), esp. chs. 3–7. For the Greek, see ed. J. G. Krabinger,

S. Gregorii Episcopi Nysseni De Anima et Resurrectionecum sorore sua Macrina dialogus: Graece et Latine (Leipzig: In Libraria Gustavi Wuttigii, 1837), pp. 3–102.

44 Rowan Williams, "Gregory of Nyssa on Mind and Passion", in eds. Lionel Wickham and Caroline P. Bammel, *Christian Faith and Greek Philosophy in Late Antiquity* (Leiden: E. J. Brill, 1993), p. 244.

45 Ibid.

46 Stanley Hauerwas, "The Sanctified Body: Why Perfection Does Not Require a 'Self' ", in *Sanctify Them in the Truth: Holiness Exemplified* (Nashville, TN: Abingdon Press, 1999), p. 89.

47 From the *Life of Macrina*, cited in Bynum, *The Resurrection of the Body*, p. 86. For the relevant passage in the Greek edition, see ed. Pierre Maraval, *Grégoire de Nysse: Vie de Sainte Macrine*, Sources Chrétiennes 178 (Paris: Éditions du Cerf, 1971), pp. 242–247.

48 Bynum, *The Resurrection of the Body*, p. 86.

49 I use the term "bowdlerized" ironically, of course, since Dr. Bowdler himself would presumably have had some difficulty trying to work out what to do with either Freud or Foucault! I mean that most popularized readings of Freud and Foucault "expurgate" not so much the sexual content of their writings but their subtler points of analysis.

50 This essay was originally presented to the annual conference of the *British Society for the Study of Theology*, Edinburgh, April 12–15, 1999. I am most grateful for the comments received there. I must also acknowledge my gratitude to my Harvard colleagues Nicholas Constas and Gary Anderson for an interesting recent cooperative Greek reading-group on the gender theory of Gregory of Nyssa.

CHAPTER 5

A MESSIAH FOR THE THIRD MILLENNIUM

DAVID F. FORD

Perhaps the most obvious historical significance of the year 2000 is that it has something to do with Jesus. In discussions about how to mark the millennium this has evoked a mixture of recognition, evasion, triumphalism, opportunism, regret, awkwardness, and some theology. In this article I will look briefly at the significance of Jesus over the past two millennia before following one particular line on the theological importance of the millennium.

1. The Significance of Jesus

Jesus is clearly of great significance by many sorts of reckoning. Today, one and a half billion people are estimated to be Christians of some sort, and there are innumerable ways in which he is significant for them. And he is significant for many others besides Christians—for example, for those affected by Christians and the Christian churches, and those who engage with him in a wide range of contexts—historical studies; religious, political or cultural studies; ethics; literature and the arts; tourism; and the considerable amount of media attention in print, radio, television, film, and the Internet. Jesus is today a world figure, not only because his followers are present in every country but also because of developments in education, travel and communications. By a crude measure of the number of occurrences of his name or of what is closely associated with his name (such as Christianity) he emerges as one of the most significant figures in the world today.

All that shows the figure of Jesus to be a remarkable phenomenon. It is worth drawing attention to it, because amidst the inundations of information pouring over us it is actually possible to miss even such largescale significance. Even reading the surface of history it is an extraordinary story.

David F. Ford
University of Cambridge Faculty of Divinity, St John's Street, Cambridge CB2 1TW, UK

An obscure Jewish rabbi became the icon of the Roman Empire and later a global figure, helping to shape the lives of billions of people. In the process there are massive conflicts, divisions and wars. In the early centuries the most bitter conflicts within the Church were over Jesus, and after the Council of Chalcedon in 451 some Churches separated. After the seventh century Jesus became a key issue between Christianity and Islam. At the end of the first millennium Eastern and Western Christianity split apart, with the relation of Jesus to his Father being the main explicit theological reason. After that, perhaps the most traumatic and certainly the most christologically explicit conflict was the splitting of the Western church in the Reformation, whose damage was immeasurably compounded by the self-discrediting of Christianity in religious wars.

Those dramatic conflicts and many other obvious manifestations of the significance of Jesus can of course give a very misleading picture. They ignore the rich, complex ways in which he has affected lives, communities and civilizations over the centuries. Least of all do they fill what counts as "significance" with appropriate theological content. It has been a story of worldly success, power and failure. Might not significance before God appear very different?

If Jesus's own teaching and example were to be the criterion might his significance be sought in things often very hard to discover historically, let alone situate in a vast overarching story? What about acts of mercy, forgiveness, patience and gentleness; the unquantifiable generosity of the widow's mite; purity of heart; willingness to fail faithfully rather than be historically successful in sinful ways? It is not hard to evoke a counter-history of significance, leading us to attend to people and events largely ignored by historians and using criteria of importance alien to most historiography. Such suspicions have in fact been common in much recent reconsideration of history. It has been one of the marks of postmodern thought at its best that it has drawn attention to obscured histories and subverted the narratives told by the victors through drawing attention to their victims. This has rightly affected the telling of Christian history too, whose origins were in the story of a victim and his persecuted followers. It raises sharply the question of the primary perspective of the story. Is it one which can do justice to the primacy of love, justice, gentleness and so on in the Christian witness? That perspective makes people in their ethical, face to face relations primary, and every other level is judged by whether it serves this. And this level is inevitably one which is largely hidden to the historian. Christology must ensure that this primacy is maintained in judging what is most significant.

I do not think that this approach invalidates the other broad-brush story, but it does supplement it, and it also sets an interrogative agenda for examining each of its periods. For my purposes here it invites consideration of an obvious, conflictual strand in the history of Christianity which combines the broad-brush and the primary perspective. That strand is the significance of the Jewishness of Jesus and in particular the deeply conflictual and often tragically violent relationship of Christianity with Judaism. Is it possible to make a theological contribution to the mending of that tradition with a view to a better third millennium?

2. Mending the Metanarrative: A Non-Supersessionist Messiah?

In listing above some major conflicts, schisms and divisions in which the figure of Jesus has played an important role, I omitted the earliest and, I suspect, the most fundamental and difficult of all: the separation of Christianity from Judaism. I do not want to rehearse the evidence now, but it is worth summarizing its main lines: with regard to the Jews, contempt, hatred, persecution, forcible conversion, misrepresentation, falsehoods, prejudice, expulsion, and murder run like a stain through century after century of Christian history. During the Shoah itself, many Christian leaders and others in good standing with their churches (Catholic, Protestant and Orthodox) actively supported the Nazis; there was massive collusion, complicity and indifference by Christians; and there was little support for the Jews from the worldwide church—the predominant reaction was silence.

The indictment could be far longer, but my point is that this was by no means unrelated to the way Jesus Christ was believed in. The opening sentence in the first chapter of Martin Gilbert's history *The Holocaust*[1] reads:

> For many centuries, primitive Christian Europe had regarded the Jew as the "Christ-killer": an enemy and a threat to be converted and so to be "saved", or to be killed; or to be expelled, or to be put to death with sword and fire.

There are many strands in the often agonized and impassioned post-Shoah debates about Jesus Christ in relation to Judaism, but here I will choose just one, that of supersessionism.

Supersessionism sees the church as superseding the Jews as the people of God. This can be accompanied by active hatred and attacks on Jews for their role in killing Christ and rejecting the Christian message, or it can encourage attempts to convert them, or it can be neutral or even benignly tolerant towards them; but the key point is that the theology of supersessionism opens the way for writing the Jews out of any positive role in the "divine economy" of history. A contemporary way of putting it might be that Judaism has generally been an anachronism in the Christian metanarrative: Jews have no good future unless they become Christians. Auschwitz can be seen as a secularized attempt to fulfil the supersessionist metanarrative, the logic of which is that there is no place for Judaism. There are, of course, many complicating factors, such as the need to issue many other indictments (against racism, militarism, nationalism, "scientism", and a range of other "modern" elements in Nazism) and the related fact that Nazi anti-semitism was not simply a version of religious anti-semitism—it eliminated converted Jews too; but the terrible truth for Christians is that the logic of their theology had fatal affinities with Nazi ideology.

The Shoah represents such a massive breakdown of Christianity that the obvious question is whether it can be repaired. George Steiner in his recent autobiography recalls his friendship with Donald MacKinnon and says:

> There could, for Donald, be no justifiable future for Christianity so long as Christian theology and practice had not faced up to, had not internalized lucidly, its seminal role in the millennial torments of Judaism and in the Holocaust.[2]

The repairs need to be multiple and they go far beyond theology; but any mending which does not tackle supersessionism is heading inevitably for further breakdown. Supersessionism is intrinsic to the Christian pathology in relating to Jews. Moreover, if supersessionism is replaced by a better theology then the implications ramify far beyond the core matter of relations between Christianity and Judaism. It is itself a vast topic, but my aim is only to sketch the bare outline of a non-supersessionist theology which is true to the New Testament.

2.1 Millennial Significance
There is a further factor which makes this a topic of special interest around the year 2000. The relationship between Jews and Christians has been a continuous strand through the past two thousand years, beginning with the birth of Christianity and culminating in the most horrific way in the twentieth century. Therefore, if one seriously wants to look back over those two millennia so as to learn lessons and try to open up a better future, this strand must be one of the main candidates for attention at this time. If one were to celebrate a date related to the beginning of Christianity, at the end of a century such as the twentieth, and *not* to attempt to come to terms with the history of Christians with Jews, that would be to betray both blindness about the past and present and irresponsibility towards the future.

The years around 2000 might even claim an importance specifically related to the Shoah: they are the last years in which there will be living witnesses of those events. This might well, if my proposal about the millennium is accepted, be the deepest significance of the year 2000: not as a round number but as the time around which the classic testimonies to the Shoah are likely to be written, or expressed in other media.

Any epochal event takes time for testimony to it to mature: the gospels could not have been written as they were immediately after the day of Pentecost. It took thirty years or more for them to be distilled in the memory; but the optimal time also did not extend much past the death of the original eyewitnesses. In an event of such proportions, the first witnesses have a special authority. It is similar with the Shoah. We are in an unrepeatable moment now, and this is confirmed both by the quality of matured testimony appearing in many forms and by the widespread interest in it. In my Faculty in Cambridge we have a course called "Jewish and Christian Responses to the Holocaust" in which I play a small part. It is a course whose atmosphere is like no other that I have taken part in. There are no doubt many reasons for that (such as participation by Jewish, Christian and Muslim teachers and students), but one is a sense that the discourse of this subject is at present in its classical formative phase and that we who engage with it have a unique historical responsibility. This time for producing and appropriately recognizing the classics of testimony, which can combine with critical inquiry what Saul Friedlander calls "deep memory", will not recur, and the urgency of the lessons which need to be learnt reinforces the pressure to be both creative and discerning. Steiner writes of MacKinnon "trying to 'think' Auschwitz and Golgotha as implicated in some interrelated finality".[3] A pressing challenge at the turn of this millennium is, therefore, to try to face the testimony to each of them as fully as possible; and part of that is facing the heritage of supersessionist Christian theology.

2.2 "He is our peace": Jews, Christians and Fulfilment

I will approach the question of supersessionism through bringing the New Testament Letter to the Ephesians into dialogue with *Peirce, Pragmatism and the Logic of Scripture* by Peter Ochs.[4]

Ephesians is chosen because its plain sense lends itself to a realized eschatology in which Jews and Gentiles are made one in the church. It is a short step to a supersessionism which sees no further role in history for the Jewish people outside the church, or at best regards Judaism as a negative shadow of Christianity. The strong emphasis on fulfilment in Ephesians reinforces this. If one links the universal scope of 1:10 (*"…* a plan for the fulness of time [*oikonomian tou pleromatos ton kairon*], to gather up all things in him [Christ], things in heaven and things on earth") with the ecclesial triumphalism of 1:22–23 ("and he [God] has put all things under his [Christ's] feet and has made him the head over all things for the church, which is his body, the fulness of him who fills all in all [*to pleroma tou ta panta en pasin pleroumenou*]"), then one can understand how Jews could easily be written out of history, with all sorts of appalling consequences when Gentiles became dominant in the church and the balance of power between Judaism and Christianity shifted in favour of the latter. Much more could be said about this, but the main point is simple: using the language of peace and unity (with differences unified within the church), Ephesians focuses in the church the fulfilment of God's *oikonomia*, and runs the danger (which has been fulfilled over and over again) of the continuing Jewish community being regarded as outside or opposed to God's *oikonomia* and therefore to be distanced, disrespected or even eliminated.

Peter Ochs' book is chosen because it is the most impressive attempt I have found to articulate a "logic of scripture" which does justice simultaneously to Jewish and Christian traditions of scriptural interpretation; to the need for each of those traditions to learn from the premodern, from the modern and from our own period (whatever label is attached to it—late modern? postmodern? submodern?); and to the urgent importance of these issues as we enter the new millennium. Ochs' thought is also deeply marked by the impact of the Shoah and by sensitivity to the multifaceted crisis which that cataclysm represents for Judaism, Christianity and Western modernity. I will not assume that readers are acquainted with Ochs' none too easy book, and so will begin with a minimal introduction to some of Ochs' ideas which will be used in the interpretation of Ephesians.

2.2.1 Introducing Ochs
The main thrust of Ochs is to show how Peirce offers a "pragmatic reading" of the modern Cartesian-Kantian philosophical tradition so as to correct and redefine it, especially through engagement with the experimental methods of the natural sciences.

One key feature of Peirce's correction is to show how that tradition's claims to discontinuity with the past were part of a misconstrual of its own nature and significance. In fact, Peirce and Ochs claim, the Cartesian-Kantian tradition is better seen as a correction of features of the tradition of medieval scholastic (and earlier) philosophy, and both traditions are to be understood in relation to "common sense". The common sense of any community needs to be open to correction, but it also contains many "indubitable beliefs" on which people act and which it is wiser to trust rather than indulge in a Cartesian principle of radical doubt. Efforts at correction should be stimulated by "real doubts"—avoiding, for example, a foundationalist attempt to meet every "paper doubt".

Failing to do justice to the tradition or community of which they are part is one aspect of a broader Cartesian-Kantian failing. This is the tendency to describe judgements, statements of fact and propositions in dyadic, subject-predicate terms rather than in a triadic logic of relations.[5] An important implication of this is that there is a "third grade of clearness" in the meaning of a conception, beyond Cartesian "clarity" and "distinctness". The third grade conceives "the practical effects which the object of a conception would have",[6] (what Peirce calls the conception's "interpretant") and includes attending to when, where, how and by whom it is received. There is here no rejection of clarity and distinctness, but a correction and supplementing of them in a way which especially insists on the significance of discourse, symbolic action and dialogue, as well as community, tradition and common sense. Many key concepts cannot be clarified in the abstract: they await further determination as they are applied or communicated in a specific context.

This leads to the helpful idea of "vagueness", which refers to a meaning which is neither determinately specific nor indeterminately general but rather only discloses its meaning by way of some interpretant.[7] Since "vague entities define one another dialogically"[8] and some concepts are "irremediably vague" (including indubitable beliefs and many other concepts concerning metaphysics, values and theology[9]), there can be no undergirding foundationalism: "a logic of vagueness is at the same time a logic of dialogue".[10]

Part of that dialogue in a tradition is its constant attempt to deal with its own problems, sufferings, contradictions, "burdensome" elements, doubts and incompleteness. "Pragmatic reading" responds to problems in the "plain sense" of the texts of a tradition by drawing on the resources of the tradition itself in order to correct or redefine it for particular readers in particular situations, taking their "common sense" both seriously and critically. Ochs describes how Peirce himself did this as he corrected and redefined his earlier "pragmatism" in his later "pragmaticism". He also shows how the logic of dialogue can (and, where the issues at stake are as embracing as those in philosophy and theology, should) lead beyond the boundaries of one tradition and bring different communities of readers into conversation.

In his final chapter Ochs promotes this by addressing various communities of pragmatic philosophers as well as Rabbinic and Christian pragmatic interpreters of scripture. He sees Rabbinic and Christian pragmatists agreeing on the need for a critique of modernist philosophy using a scriptural corrective and also on the need for "a reformational reading of scripture" which rereads "scriptural texts as vague symbols of rules of conduct that are defined only in specific contexts of action within respective communities of readers".[11] He then urges that they each need to be in dialogue with each other, and concludes with guidelines for such a dialogue.

I am here trying to contribute to a Christian understanding of the Letter to the Ephesians that grapples with the problems and vagueness of that letter at the turn of the millennium, dialogue between Christians and Jews being of special concern.[12]

2.2.2 The Question of Peace

"[T]he pragmatic meaning of a conception is the sum total of its practical consequences for the long run of experience ..."[13] How might that maxim relate to Ephesians 2:14: "For he is our peace, in his flesh he has made both groups into one, and has broken down the dividing wall, that is, the hostility between us"? The reference is to Jews and Gentiles, and in view of "the long run of experience" over nearly two thousand years it must constitute a major problem for the interpretation of Ephesians today. If pragmatic scriptural reading aims to read "in response to human suffering" and "with a community of readers for the sake of changing the practical and communal conditions of suffering",[14] then in view of the terrible history of Christian persecution of Jews there is a need for correction of Christian conceptions of

Jews. The constructive question is whether there might be a valid and strong reading of Ephesians which not only resists Christian hostility to Jews but even allows the communities today to be of mutual blessing. How might this tradition not only correct itself but even surpass itself with the aid of "plain sense" and "pragmatic" readings of Ephesians?

2.2.3 Resources in the Plain Sense of Ephesians

Might the plain sense of Ephesians itself resist the danger of supersessionism? Are there materials for the correction of this tendency of the tradition? The most obvious resistance comes in the ethics of Ephesians. It is an ethic of non-coercive communication, of speaking the truth in love (4:15), of "all humility and gentleness, with patience, bearing with one another in love" (4:2). If such speech and action were to characterize relations with those outside as well as inside the community then, whatever the beliefs about Jews in relation to God's *oikonomia*, there would be respect, communication and peace. The root of this resistance within Ephesians is in who Jesus Christ is believed to be. All the uniting, fulfilling and peacemaking is seen as being done through someone who embodies love, gentleness, patience and giving up self for others without limit (cf. 4:31, 5:1–2).

It is also worth remembering the probable context into which the letter was written: a small, vulnerable church in a thriving, pluralist city of about a quarter of a million people where there were a great many more Jews than Christians. The letter shows that this church clearly needed great encouragement and a strengthening of its identity, and what was appropriate then and there might not be so in another situation.

Yet none of that is good enough. It might expose how much Christian treatment of Jews has been unethical by Christian standards, and it might contextualize the rhetoric of Ephesians so that its statements cannot simply be turned into general guidelines from which all sorts of new conclusions can be drawn directly in new situations; but it fails to tackle the issue of the prominence of Jews and Gentiles in the letter, in which peace between them is made central to the *musterion* of the Gospel, and it ignores the basic theological issue of supersessionism. How might this be faced?

First, it is to be noted that Ephesians itself can be read as correcting and redefining the Pauline Christian tradition. It is generally seen as dependent on the Letter to the Colossians (out of 2,411 words in Ephesians, 26.5% are paralleled in Colossians, once with 29 consecutive words repeated verbatim), so it is especially interesting to note where the two diverge. Among the notable divergences are the two themes of peace and fulfilment. The Colossians themes of the church as the body of Christ and of "peace through the blood of his [Christ's] cross" are developed by Ephesians into an explicit focus on peace between Jews and Gentiles in the church. And the Colossians theme of *pleroma* (the fulness of God dwelling in Christ—1:19, 2:9) is maintained and intensified in its cosmic scope and its relation to Christian living, and developed explicitly in relation to "the fulness of time" (1:10), the church, and love in the community (3:14–21).

There are many directions the discussion of this could take—deeper into the comparison and contrast of Ephesians and Colossians; backwards, especially to Paul in his Letter to the Romans; forwards to later Christian writers; and backwards, forwards and sideways into Jewish and Hellenistic contexts. But for present purposes it is enough to try to identify with a broad brush the significance of what Ephesians has done. It has intensified the universality of its conception of fulfilment (frequent use of "all", "all things", "everyone") at the same time as intensifying the particularity of the community's *musterion*, defined as: "... that is, the Gentiles have become fellow heirs, members of the same body, and sharers in the promise in Christ Jesus through the Gospel" (3:6). This particularity is reinforced in Ephesians through far more use of the Septuagint than in Colossians. It is crucial to note the sort of unity described between Jews and Gentiles: the Gentiles are given the privilege of sharing a Jewish heritage. This heritage is the unsurpassable horizon of the church. That is where Ephesians leaves the matter: the conjunction of, on the one hand, a universalizing soteriology of abundant reconciliation, peace and love, to be completed in "the fulness of time", with, on the other hand, a small community in which the *musterion* of unity between Jews and Gentiles was a reality. The two dimensions are embraced by Jesus Christ, as the one in whom all things are gathered, and the Holy Spirit, as "the pledge of our inheritance toward redemption as God's own people, to the praise of his glory" (1:14).

Yet after all that, the massive problem remains: what about those of "God's own people" who do not acknowledge Jesus Christ in the way the author does?

2.2.4 Pleroma in Ephesians: A Pragmatic Reading

In Ochs' terms, I have identified "something burdensome in the plain sense"[15] of Ephesians. This now stimulates me to suggest what he calls a midrashic, or pragmatic interpretation. As he says, such a reading is to be judged by how well it resolves the given problem "for a given community of interpreters"[16]—in my case, Christian interpreters who are in dialogue with Jews at the end of a century marked by the Shoah. What might be the "non-evident meaning"[17] of Ephesians on this matter in line with the leading tendencies of the letter?

In this case, the problem is not mainly in what Ephesians says explicitly. It lies more in its "pragmatic meaning" in the millennia that followed—though in fact for many Christians the problematic reading has been read as the plain sense and has shaped their "common sense". Ochs might say that the "irremediably vague" concept of *pleroma* was later given overprecise ("errantly clear") pragmatic definitions which were decisively supersessionist and ruled out any continuing positive role of Jews in God's *oikonomia*, with disastrous implications. An appropriate response to this is to offer a better (in Ochs' terms, a more valid and stronger) pragmatic definition.

What might that be? I will only sketch some of the elements of a possible pragmatic reading. They will be in the form of questions and notes focussed as commentary on particular verses in which the noun or verb form of *pleroma* appears.

2.2.4.1 Ephesians 1:9–10

[With all wisdom and insight God] has made known to us the mystery of his will, according to his good pleasure that he set forth in Christ, as a plan for the fulness of time, to gather up all things in him, things in heaven and things on earth.

How is this gathering up to be envisaged? If it is done with wisdom, love and gentleness, aiming at what seems inconceivable when we look at the fragmentations, divisions, wounds and enmities of the world, then we have to imagine boundaries of selves and communities radically transformed. If the horizon of their Jewish heritage is unsurpassable for Christians, and if, for both Jews and Christians, practical orientation towards an utterly good "fulness of time" has the status of an "indubitable belief", which is "irremediably vague", then the implications of a logic of vagueness being "at the same time a logic of dialogue"[18] must mean that there is a dialogical imperative here. Christians trust that fulfilment is in the hands of Jesus Christ, but they have no privileged overview of its details—in fact its "vagueness" and universal scope means that it constantly calls for further determinations from a wide range of interpretants. So the pragmatic reading of these verses will lead into a range of respectful dialogues (not just between Jews and Christians, but with Muslims, atheists, and others) as well as into all sorts of other activities that "gathering up all things" might require—the arts, scholarship, the sciences, economics, politics and so on. And part of the appropriate vagueness is allowing for transformative surprises.

2.2.4.2 Ephesians 1:22–3

And [God] has put all things under [Christ's] feet and has made him head over all things for the church, which is his body, the fulness of him who fills all in all.

If 1:10 makes clear that the fulness has yet to be completed, then the nature of the eschatological community is a fascinating question. How does it relate to present Christian and Jewish and other communities? Eugene Rogers, following on from George Lindbeck's contention that both the church and Israel should be regarded as types, not of Christ, but of "the people of God in fellowship with God at the end of time",[19] makes a convincing case for the contribution of an "anagogical" interpretation of scripture, reading it in the light of the eschatological community. His own anagogical reading of Romans Chapters 9–11 (which is strikingly "pragmatic" in Ochs' terms) is in line with Ephesians: the basic plot is a Jewish one oriented towards consummation, with Gentile redemption a sub-plot. God's faithfulness to the covenant with Israel is permanent. There "are not two stories, much less two covenants, but two ways the Spirit excites gratitude for the blessings of Abraham in the readers of the bible, who in this too can become sources of mutual blessing."[20] And it is worth remembering that there are many other Gentiles besides Christians.

2.2.4.3 Ephesians 3:18–20

I pray that you may have the power to comprehend, with all the saints, what is the breadth and length and height and depth, and to know the love of Christ that surpasses knowledge, so that you may be filled with all the fulness of God. Now to him who by the power at work within us is able to accomplish abundantly far more than all we can ask or imagine ...

God is the most important consideration of all in relation to *pleroma*. This prayer acknowledges that, it denies that Christians or others have an overview of the meaning of *pleroma*, and in Ochs' terms the text is "an ultimately vague sign of the God whose activities correct it and clarify its meaning".[21] The meaning of "fulness" has to take into account the infinite dynamic abundance of a God of love, fulfilling prayers in ways we could never have imagined. The God identified here questions many of the terms and presuppositions in which Christian supersessionism has been expressed—concerning linearity, binary oppositions, completeness, closure, the boundaries of communities, election and salvation—and all of those would need further discussion in a full theological treatment.

2.2.4.4 Ephesians 4:13

... until all of us come to the unity of the faith and of the knowledge of the Son of God, to maturity, to the measure of the full stature [*eis helikias tou pleromatos*] of Christ.

Ephesians Chapters 4–6 is about some of the communal, personal and institutional practices which are involved in interpreting *pleroma*. The idea of "learning Christ" is used (4:20), and, pragmatically understood, that conjures up a vast, complex learning process (including much "unlearning"), involving exchanges with individuals, communities and disciplines that are part of the "gathering together" of 1:10, and shaping habits accordingly. "Learning Christ" might be seen as the basic continuing relationship to the Messiah.

2.2.4.5 Ephesians 5:18–20

> Do not get drunk with wine, for that is debauchery; but be filled [*plerousthe*] with the Spirit, as you sing psalms and hymns and spiritual songs among yourselves, singing and making melody to the Lord in your hearts, giving thanks to God the Father at all times and for everything in the name of our Lord Jesus Christ.

Ephesians is saturated with praise and prayer, and this imperative about the shaping of ordinary life is vital for working out practically the implications of *pleroma*. The logic of praise as perfecting what is perfect, the logic of thanks as completing what is completed, and the similar logic of blessing: it is these, learnt and practised daily over centuries, that need to inform understanding of and participation in *pleroma*.[22]

2.2.5 A Non-Supersessionist Christ

Yet, as those centuries also demonstrate, those very dynamics can also go terribly wrong. So it is salutary to try to learn disciplines of reading which encourage facing up to the burdens, failings, errors, sufferings, and remediable or irremediable vaguenesses occasioned by interpretations of scripture. One of the strengths of Ochs' approach is that it both encourages a tradition to find within itself the resources for its own correction and redefinition, and also to "believe that, through the mediation of particular community members, communities of scriptural reading may themselves enter into dialogues that strengthen each community's practices of reading by complementing and clarifying them".[23] That is what Ochs has assisted me in attempting, and I hope that the suggested plain sense and pragmatic readings of Ephesians help towards a non-supersessionist conception of Jesus Christ for the new millennium which not only contributes to the mending of the Christian tradition but also opens up constructive possibilities for Christian relations with Jews and others.

3. A Messiah Facing Auschwitz[24]

In his 1997 Cardinal Bea Memorial Lecture, Rabbi Dr Nicholas de Lange[25] sees the Shoah as the third *churban*—the others being the Babylonian exile and the Roman destruction of the Temple in 70 A.D. He calls it a twentieth century Calvary and reads the Gospels as post-Holocaust literature, with the cross being a symbol or allegory of the Shoah. He speaks of Jewish wrestling with the question: "Where was God at Auschwitz?" and throws out a challenge:

> We have reached the point now, I believe, where we cannot engage in meaningful dialogue with any Christian who has not similarly confronted the question: "Where was Jesus Christ at Auschwitz?"[26]

He sharpens this by a series of disturbing quotations from Dietrich Bonhoeffer, Martin Niemöller and Jürgen Moltmann,[27] and a vivid evocation of the crucified Jesus as the persecutor of his own people:

It is painful to contemplate the thought of those pierced hands dripping with the spilt blood of so many innocent victims.[28]

A Christian response to that cannot treat the crucifixion of Jesus as nothing but symbol or allegory; but nor can it treat Auschwitz as illustrating or symbolizing the crucifixion. MacKinnon saw them as implicated in some "interrelated finality", and it is one which does not permit over-views or integrations. How can they be thought together in Christian theology?

As soon as the question is raised its implications ramify through many areas of theology. I want to suggest as a starting-point a statement of Christian faith: Jesus Christ was facing Auschwitz.

Elsewhere I have outlined a theology of the face and facing of Jesus Christ.[29] It is a theology which, in line with mainstream Christianity, would affirm about Auschwitz as about other events that Jesus Christ was present to it (requiring treatment of issues of God, evil, death, absence, resurrection, selfhood, and so on). There are those for whom Auschwitz makes such an affirmation incredible, especially if it is accompanied by any trust or hope in Jesus Christ as saviour. That is an argument which would require far more space than is available here;[30] my concern now is to ask not whether a Christian answer can be shown to be convincing in debate with others but whether it might even make sense.

Jesus Christ facing the Shoah evokes simultaneously a double inquiry: interrogative faith before the face of one who was a baby, ate, drank, taught, proclaimed the Kingdom of God, was transfigured, prayed in Gethsemane, was kissed by Judas, was arrested, tried, flogged, crucified, and rose from the dead; and seeking understanding before the faces of the victims, of the perpetrators, of the silent and speaking witnesses, and of others. What it means to face Auschwitz in this sense can be entered into through testimonies in many media and genres. Anyone immersed in the double testimony to Golgotha and to Auschwitz is likely to be stretched past their capacity in study, imagination and feeling to do justice to the Shoah and to God in relation to it. But above all faith is exercised in practical response before one who is believed both to take radical responsibility for the world, to the point of death, and also to call others into comparable responsibility. What this should involve for the Church and its theology after Auschwitz has hardly begun to be faced, but clearly should be a Christian priority for the new millennium.

To be before this face that has witnessed Auschwitz is to be summoned to face Auschwitz in his spirit and to be called to accept responsibility for such things not happening again. It is to follow his gaze not only towards the victims, perpetrators and innocent or guilty bystanders of the Shoah but towards other sufferers and victims. It is also to be encouraged to trust that the Shoah and other evils are not the last word about human life.

But how might this theology of the face of Christ avoid being dominating, triumphalist, exclusivist, supersessionist and other bad things? Christian theology has often been rightly subject to such accusations and suspicions. Yet the face and facing of Jesus Christ might also hold the possibility of an alternative which helps Christian theology to be both radically self-critical in facing its own past and present, and also dialogical with others. What follows is just a set of headlines for what this might be like.

The very idea of facing can be seen as resistant to totalizing overviews and syntheses. This particular face can be seen as challenging Christian (and other) ideologies of domination and coercive practices. It is the face of one who is silent, who listens to cries, who is judging yet self-effacing, suffers violence, and dies. It represents a continual critique of power in the interests of the weak and suffering, an ethic of gentleness and being for others, and forms of communication that have the crucifixion as their central criterion and dialogue as their central practice. To face Jesus Christ means learning to be responsible before him, learning to be judged by him, to look on others as he looks on them, to be vigilant, and to speak and be silent in his Spirit. To look to this face is to be before a Jew who teaches the message of the Kingdom of God and summons to seeking it as one's life-shaping desire. It is to follow his gaze of love towards his own people.

It is also to be open to radical surprise. Christians have no overview of how Jesus Christ relates to other Christians or even themselves, let alone to Jews, Muslims, Hindus, agnostics, atheists and so on. Christians trust that he relates in ways that are good beyond anything they or anyone can imagine. But what about Jews who reject him as Messiah and await the true Messiah? Neither can claim a total overview. Both Jews and Christians affirm in radical ways that the category of "surprise" is inseparable from eschatology. If anything is clear from Jesus's own teaching about God's future it is that those who are most confident that they have it worked out are likely to be most surprised. This above all is the place for reserve, for an agnostic yet expectant silence which is open to the unexpected. It is an expectancy to be filled with the prayer, vigilance, love and service which are the practical forms of anticipating the good surprise of welcome by the Messiah who is now met with incognito in responding to others. In line with the kenotic, servant character of Jesus Christ, his crucifixion and resurrection may be seen as in the service of his desire for the Kingdom of God. They are meant to send his followers back into historical existence to seek the Kingdom of God. They intensify the urgency of the ethics of the Kingdom and its teaching of a self-effacing, incognito Messiah.

De Lange's lecture ends, on the basis of his very different reading of the Gospel from mine, with a message of collaboration:

This post-Holocaust reading of the Gospel strengthens me in my belief that Jews and Christians must labour together to make certain that such a *churban* cannot happen again.[31]

He had opened his lecture with a quotation from Franz Rosenzweig:

Before God, Jew and Christian both labour at the same task. He cannot dispense with either.[32]

That sums up well the practical lesson of the non-supersessionist theology outlined above; and in addition, in that phrase "before God", which resonates for Rosenzweig with the pervasive biblical theme of the face of God that he makes so pivotal to his theology, there is an embracing horizon for our facing and being faced. The differences between Jews and Christians remain stubborn, but there is a massive common task for the new millennium.

NOTES

1   Martin Gilbert, *The Holocaust, The Jewish Tragedy* (London: Collins, 1986), p. 18.
2   George Steiner, *Errata. An examined life* (New Haven and London: Yale University Press, 1997), p. 152.
3   Ibid.
4   Cambridge: Cambridge University Press, 1998.
5   Ibid., pp. 254ff.
6   Ibid., p. 36, Ochs quoting Peirce.
7   Ibid., p. 37.
8   Ibid., p. 211.
9   Ibid., p. 226.
10 Ibid.
11 Ibid., pp. 310f.
12 An earlier version of this interpretation of Ephesians was delivered to a gathering of Christian, Jewish, Muslim and other scholars at a meeting of the Society for Scriptural Reasoning at the Annual Meeting of the American Academy of Religion in Orlando, Florida, November 1998, and I am most grateful for the responses of those who heard and discussed it there.
13 Ibid., p. 113.
14 Ibid., p. 313.
15 Ibid., p. 6.
16 Ibid., p. 7.
17 Ibid., p. 6.
18 Ibid., p. 226.
19 Eugene F. Rogers, Jr., "Supplementing Barth on Jews and Gender: Identifying God by Anagogy and the Spirit", *Modern Theology* Vol. 14 No. 1, January 1998, p. 63.
20 Ibid., p. 64.
21 Ochs, *op. cit.*, p. 287. Cf. the continuation of this passage: "By the logic of pragmatism, a vague sign 'reserves for some other sign or experience the function of completing [its] determination' (5.505). Therefore, if God is the object of an ultimately vague sign, then whatever defines this sign would also be vague, and only god would complete the determination of the sign of God."
22 For a reading of Ephesians which takes these verses as its hermeneutical key see David F. Ford, *Self and Salvation: Being Transformed* (Cambridge: Cambridge University Press, 1999) Chapter 5 "Communicating God's Abundance: A Singing Self".

23 Ochs, *op. cit.*, p. 314.
24 This section draws on a fuller treatment of this theme "Silence and the Shoah: Where was Jesus Christ at Auschwitz?" in *Silence and the Word*, edited by Oliver Davies and Denys Turner (Cambridge: Cambridge University Press, forthcoming).
25 Nicholas de Lange, "Jesus Christ and Auschwitz", *New Blackfriars* Vol. 78 No. 917/918, (July/August 1997), pp. 308–316.
26 Ibid., p. 309.
27 Professor Moltmann has said to me that he considers himself to have been misinterpreted by Dr de Lange.
28 Ibid., p. 311.
29 David F. Ford, *Self and Salvation: Being Transformed* (Cambridge: Cambridge University Press, 1999).
30 Many of the elements of my response to it are in *Self and Salvation, op. cit.*
31 "Jesus Christ and Auschwitz" *op. cit.*, p. 315.
32 Ibid., p. 308.

CHAPTER 6

THE FINAL RECONCILIATION: REFLECTIONS ON A SOCIAL DIMENSION OF THE ESCHATOLOGICAL TRANSITION

MIROSLAV VOLF

The Last Judgment—the Final Reconciliation

When asked, whether it is true that one day in heaven we will see again our loved ones, Karl Barth is reported to have responded, "Not only the loved ones!" The sting of the great theologian's response—be ready to meet there even those whom you dislike here—is more than just a personal challenge. It contains a serious and, as it turns out, inadequately addressed theological problem. How can those who have disliked or even had good reasons to hate each other here, come to inhabit together what is claimed to be, in Jonathan Edwards' memorable phrase, "a world of love"?[1] The not-loved-ones will have to be transformed into the loved ones and those who do not love will have to begin to do so; enemies will have to become friends.

A sense that such a social transformation is a condition of "heavenly" existence may lie behind a funeral practice in Germany in which a kind of a post-mortem reconciliation between the deceased and their enemies is enacted in the form of prayer. Participants in the burial service remember before God those whom the deceased may have wronged or who may have wronged them.[2] Popular piety is also aware of the issue. In tightly knit Christian communities one sometimes hears the injunction that their members had better learn to love each other now since they will spend eternity together. Sometime between a shadowy history and eternity bathed in light, somewhere between this world and the coming world of perfect love, a transformation of persons and their complex relationships needs to take

Miroslav Volf
Yale Divinity School, 409 Prospect Street, New Haven, CT 06511, USA

place. Without such transformation the world to come would not be a world of perfect love but just a repetition of a world in which, at best, the purest of loves falter and, at worst, cold indifference reigns and deadly hatreds easily flare up.

Traditionally, the last judgment along with the resurrection of the dead was taken to be the site of the eschatological transition from this world to the world to come. But if the need for transformation of persons as well as of their complex relationships is a real one, the question is whether the last judgment, as usually conceived, can carry this weight. Consider Augustine, whose thought is particularly pertinent not only because his eschatology shaped significantly the later tradition[3] but because he uses the metaphor "peace", including social peace,[4] to describe the world to come and contrasts it to the violence of the kingdoms of this world. As he defines it in *The City of God*, the peace of the coming world is "perfectly ordered and harmonious enjoyment of God and of one another in God".[5] Notice, however, how Augustine describes the eschatological transition from the world of violence to the world of peace. "Now, it is through the last judgment that men pass to these ends, the good to the supreme good, the evil to the supreme evil",[6] writes Augustine. The last judgment is a divine act directed toward individuals which definitively executes the division of humanity into damned and saved and apportions appropriate rewards and punishments. If one operates, however, with a robust notion of social peace at whose center is the enjoyment of one another in God, as Augustine does, then it is easy to see how the last judgment can be indispensable to such a peace but difficult to see how it can be sufficient to usher it in.

According to Augustine, the last judgment concerns primarily matters of justice;[7] it separates "the good" and "the bad"[8] and ensures that "the true and full happiness" be "the lot of none but the good" and "deserved and supreme misery" be "the portion of the wicked, and of them only".[9] Unless, contrary to Augustine's claim, the good are already creatures of perfect love, the execution of such justice will not make them love in the world to come those whom they may not have loved now.[10] Granted, for Augustine the last judgment is but *one* aspect of the eschatological transition toward heavenly peace. Another is the resurrection—an aspect of the ontological *novum* that a comprehensive *transformatio mundi* represents—which heals the weakness of the flesh and clothes the person in *immortalitas* and *incorruptio*.[11] The last judgment and the *transformatio mundi* together would create sufficient conditions for mutual human enjoyment; together they are meant not only to make perfect love possible, but sin impossible. The two would indeed be all we need if the eschatological transition were a creation of a brand new world of love, rather than a transformation of the existing world of enmity into a world of love. But the contrary is the case. Unlike the present world, the world to come will not be created *ex nihilo* but *ex vetere*.[12] Hence either only those who are already fully reconciled in this world could be admitted into the coming world or the reconciliation would have to occur as part of the eschatological transition itself. The first option seems excluded by Augustine's belief that one cannot have complete peace in this life.[13] The second, which Augustine does not explore,[14] needs to be developed if the eschatological transition is to reorder human relations such that human beings enjoy not only God but also one another.

Whereas justice is central in Augustine's theology of the last judgment, grace is central in Martin Luther's. The thought of judgment according to works is present, but it is integrated into the overarching judgment of grace.[15] For believers, the last judgment is not so much a process by which the moral quality of human deeds is made unmistakably manifest and appropriate rewards and punishments apportioned, but above all an event in which sinners are forgiven and justified. Christ the final judge is none other than Christ the merciful savior. "To me", writes Luther, "he is a physician, helper, and deliverer from death and the devil."[16] The Johannine Jesus says, "anyone who comes to me I will never drive away" (John 6:37). Luther interprets him to mean,

> Let it be your one concern to come to Me and to have the grace to hold, to believe, and to be sure in your heart that I was sent into the world for your sake, that I carried out the will of My Father and was sacrificed for your atonement, righteousness, sanctification, and redemption, and bore all punishment for you. If you believe this, do not fear. I do not want to be your judge, executioner, or jailer, but your Savior and Mediator, yes, your kind, loving Brother and good Friend. But you must abandon your work-righteousness and remain with Me in firm faith.[17]

Divine judgment at the end of history completes divine justification, grounded in Christ's redemptive work, in the middle of history.[18]

Yet it is not clear how the final justification of the ungodly would *as such* create a world of love—not even if we take it to include what Friedrich Schleiermacher has called "complete sanctification".[19] No doubt, it would ensure that we would meet in the world to come even those whom we have not considered particularly lovable in the present one. But for us to *love* the unlovable, two things would need to happen. First, in a carefully specified sense we ourselves would need to "justify" them, and, given that they may consider us no more lovable than we consider them, they would also need to "justify" us, and we all would need to receive this "justification" from each other.[20] Second, above and beyond giving and receiving justification, we would also need to want be in communion with one another. To usher in a world of love, the eschatological transition would need to be understood not only as a divine act toward human beings but also as *a social event between human beings*, more precisely, a divine act toward human beings which is also a social event between them. Or so I would like to argue in this essay.

Put in the form of a question about the perpetrator and the victim of the first violence in primal history, the subject I will explore is this: If Cain and Abel were to meet again in the world to come, what will need to have happened between them for Cain not to keep avoiding Abel's look and for Abel not to want to get out of Cain's way? Put in a form of a thesis, the argument I will develop is this: If the world to come is to be a world of love, then the eschatological transition from the present world to that world, which God will accomplish, must have an inter-human side; the work of the Spirit in the consummation[21] includes not only the resurrection of the dead and the last judgment but also the final social reconciliation.

The thesis is novel, or at least severely under-emphasized and under-developed. Some contemporary theologians have come close to advocating it, however. Reflecting on the shape of social relations in the world to come, Friedrich Mildenberger suggests in his *Biblische Dogmatik* that we think of the last judgment as an act of purging, in which aspects of human relationships compatible with the perfected world remain and those incompatible burn up. In some ways, this is a contemporary restatement of the notion of judgment as purification rather than punishment, prevalent in the Eastern tradition. Mildenberger understands the eschatological purification, however, against the background of socially constructed identities. Since human identities are shaped by relationships and since relationships can be freighted with evil, for the perfect sociality to emerge evil residues of relationships must be removed for the perfect sociality to emerge.[22] He seems to imply, however, that the removal of sin can take place without the involvement of people who stood in those relationships, a kind of divine readjustment of individual identities structurally comparable to the one expressed in the image of earthly attachments being scraped off the soul as it is drawn to God, which Gregory of Nyssa employs in *On the Soul and the Resurrection*.[23] But to concentrate exclusively on individuals and disregard their relationships is to sacrifice in the account of the way a person is freed from sin the fundamental insight into how the identity of a human being as a person and as a sinner is constructed. If identities are constructed and have been injured in a social process, should then not their healing, too, involve a social process, even if one grants that much of the healing can happen internally to an individual person?

Wolfhart Pannenberg seems implicitly to advocate the equivalent of what I call "the final reconciliation". Exploring how antagonisms between the individual and society will be overcome in the world to come, he writes in *Systematic Theology*, "God is the future of the finite from which it again receives its existence as a whole as that which has been, and at the same time accepts all other creaturely being along with itself."[24] The reception of one's own existence as perfected by God must go hand in hand with the acceptance of others. To be eschatologically fruitful, the notion of acceptance, which Pannenberg only suggests, would need to be unpacked and its full social and temporal dimensions elaborated. But the notion points in the right direction because it implies that before the antagonism between individual and society can be overcome—before the world of love can be created—*relationships* between human beings must be transformed.[25]

My argument that the final social reconciliation is an integral element of the Spirit's work in the consummation will proceed in three simple steps. First, I will examine one notable example of "the final reconciliation" in philosophical literature—Socrates' comments about the last judgment in *Phaedo*—and via an appreciative critique of Socrates lay the groundwork for my own proposal. Second, I will offer positive theological reasons for advocating "the final social reconciliation" by relating it to the nature of human beings, the character of sin, and the shape of salvation. Finally, I will engage two questions which provide critical test cases for the plausibility of the thesis: (1) whether it is compatible with the affirmations that human beings were reconciled with one another in Christ and (2) that the subject of the eschatological transition is God rather than human beings. Before embarking upon my journey I should note that, though a particular notion of the last judgment is central to my arguments, I am able to develop the notion of the last judgment in this text only as it relates directly to the final social reconciliation.

Victims' Mercy—Perpetrators' Salvation

One rare but notable philosophical text which advocates the possibility and the need of a post-mortem reconciliation is the "eschatological myth" in Plato's *Phaedo*. As I will elaborate shortly, many aspects of that myth are theologically problematic. Christian theology will do well, however, to appropriate, reformulate, and develop some of its basic insights. Before engaging the text, I ought to clarify a hermeneutical question. I will eschew the debate of Plato scholars about the proper interpretation of the "mythical" character of the text. It is not clear in the dialogue how precisely the mythic "tale" relates to the preceding arguments. Socrates himself says that, though the tale of "the soul and her mansions" is not "exactly true", "inasmuch as the soul is shown to be immortal", we may "venture to think, not improperly or unworthily, that something of the kind is true".[26] Given that Socrates has *argued* for the immortality of the soul, and therefore for a particular "nature of the pilgrimage" which he was "about to make",[27] I will take him at his word and interpret the myth as a narratival rendering, made necessary by the limitations of discursive analysis,[28] of a future afterlife, rather than, for example, primarily an image of the present life.[29]

Toward the end of the eschatological myth Socrates, who is about to execute on himself the sentence of death by drinking poison, tells his friends about the sentences the dead will have passed on them when they "arrive at the place to which the genius ... conveys them". Of the five groups in which he divides humanity, the sentences for four groups are predictable, more or less. Those "who appear to be incurable by reason of the greatness of their crime" are "hurled into Tartarus" ("a chasm which pierces right through the whole earth"[30]) "which is their suitable destiny, and they never come out". Those "who appear to have lived neither well nor ill"—the great majority of people[31]—are "purified of their evil deeds" and "receive the rewards of their good deeds according to their deserts". Those "who have been preeminent for holiness of life" are "released from their earthly prison, and go to their pure home which is above, and dwell in the purer earth". Finally, those who "have duly purified themselves with philosophy, live henceforth altogether without the body, in mansions fairer far than these, which may not be described".[32]

Sandwiched between the third and fourth is the last group, whose sentence Socrates expounds most extensively. The group comprises those "who have committed crimes, which, although great, are not irremediable", such as those "who in a moment of anger, for example, have done some violence to a father or a mother and have repented for the remainder of their lives, or, who have taken the life of another under the like extenuating circumstances". Their sentence seems unusual at first sight and questionable in many of its aspects, but is nonetheless in some ways profoundly right. Here is how Socrates describes it:

> ... these are plunged into Tartarus, the pains of which they are compelled to undergo for a year, but at the end of the year the wave casts them forth—mere homicides by way of [the river] Cocytus, parricides and matricides by Pyriphlegethon—and they are borne to the Acherusian lake, and there they lift up their voices and call upon their victims whom they have slain or wronged, to have pity on them, and to be kind to them, and let them come out into the lake. And if they prevail, then they come forth and cease from their troubles; but if not, they are carried back again into Tartarus and from thence into the rivers unceasingly, until they obtain mercy from those whom they have wronged; for that is the sentence inflicted upon them by their judges.

A possible healing of a particular kind of perpetrator, Socrates suggests, depends not only on the purgatorial pain suffered and on the perpetrator's plea for mercy, but also on the willingness of their victims to show mercy.

It is easy to locate the spots at which Socrates' account of "the last judgment", and in particular of the sentence for curable souls, is problematic,[33] at least from a Christian perspective. I will leave aside here, for instance, his well known privileging of a bodiless state in which a soul can comprehend Ideas as such, and not as they are immanent in sensible particulars; it does not rhyme with the resurrection of the body. Instead, I will concentrate on issues which concern the general character of the judgment and the specific sentence of curable souls. As will be evident, my perspective is decisively shaped by a theological tradition with some reservations about the traditional notions of purgatory.

First, Socrates operates with what might be described as a mirroring relation between pre-mortem and post-mortem life. The soul is judged "on the basis of its degree of goodness while the soul animated the human body"; the task of the judge is simply to "ratify" the soul's moral status.[34] Especially since Luther, in Christian theology, on the other hand, the judgment is fundamentally a saving event, at least for the blessed. Second, Socrates believes that there are crimes so heinous as to render those who committed them incurable and that there are lives so pure as to earn those who led them mansions beyond description. In the Christian tradition no deed is imaginable that would as such hurl a person of necessity (Socrates' "destiny") into damnation, for the simple reason that deeds are not decisive when it comes to afterlife;[35] inversely, no deed and therefore no life is so holy or pure as to qualify a person for entry into heavenly bliss. Finally, when Socrates contemplates betterment for evildoers in the post-mortem state, change always involves pain inflicted from the outside and understood as a form of purification. Though in the traditional Catholic doctrine of purgatory, "physical" pain is seen as a form of purification, Protestant theology has emphasized transformation as a sheer gift of God involving no other suffering than the pain of self-discovery. All three points amount to a fundamental difference in the character of the last judgment.[36] For Socrates, the last judgment is situated in an economy of deserts; in the next life everyone gets what they have deserved in this life. In Christian theology, the last judgment is situated in an economy of grace—grace, however, which does not negate justice but affirms it precisely in the act of transcending it.[37]

The only place where Socrates seems to step out of the economy of deserts —though with one foot only, so to speak—is in the treatment of curable souls. They, too, suffer so as to be purified, but the suffering is not sufficient to change their lot. The perpetrators need to be shown mercy by the victims to be admitted to further purification and finally "sent back" (admittedly only "to be born as animals").[38] But here a major problem with Socrates' scheme surfaces. As one commentator notes, in Socrates' proposal everything depends on the "chance factors of the victim's sense of mercy and the wrongdoers' powers of rhetoric".[39] Surely something is amiss if two perpetrators commit comparable crimes but the one with a smooth tongue whose victim is merciful gets off the hook while the less eloquent one whose victim is vengeful suffers the consequences!

Part of the problem is that Socrates has arranged things in such a way that the perpetrator and the victim have to sort out *by themselves* the issues between them. A third party, the judges, only defines the process and sets it in motion. The judges' standing on the sidelines is in fact part of the sentence. In the absence of an appropriate third party arbitrariness reigns. It is not clear, for instance, at what point the unwillingness of the victim to offer mercy and deliver the perpetrator from Tartarus turns into vindictiveness. Furthermore, though a "mechanism" is in place by which a perpetrator can be purified, Socrates does not even reflect on the possible need for the victim to be transformed, for instance, to be freed from bitterness and vindictiveness.

The problematic character of the judgment as a whole and of the sentence inflicted on curable souls notwithstanding, profound eschatological insights are contained in the sentence. I am thinking of its two central and inter-related features. First, *the action of the third party, though indispensable, is alone not sufficient to deal with the problem.* Socrates is aware of the perverse inter-personal bond that violence suffered creates between the perpetrator and the victim. For the perpetrator to be released, something needs to happen *between* the perpetrator and the victim, not just *in* each of them (for instance, repentance, in the case of the perpetrator, or inner healing, in the case of the victim). Without a particular kind of interaction between them it is difficult to imagine the perpetrator's restoration. Second, *justice understood as desert does not suffice to restore the perpetrator.* Though justice is indispensable, re-quired also are the psychological and interpersonal phenomena of repentance and forgiveness, of a sense of guilt and the offer of mercy.

Socrates seemed concerned primarily with the fate of the perpetrator as an individual; his or her reintegration into community is not so much in view (though if one were to make a somewhat daring hermeneutical leap and read Socrates' statement in *Phaedo* against the backdrop of the Athenian Stranger's laws for dealing with pollution from involuntary murder in Plato's *Laws*—a period of exile and readmission into the society[40]—a vision of reconciliation between the perpetrator and the victim would be implied). If the interaction between the two in the form of a request for forgiveness and offer of mercy is essential for healing of the perpetrator, it is *a fortiori* essential for the *restoration of the relationship between them and the creation of the community of unmarred and unadulterated love.* I propose therefore that we take up Socrates' two basic insights about the healing of curable souls—the indispensability of a social process and the insufficiency of justice conceived as desert—and place them in the context of an economy of grace, which governs Christian soteriology and eschatology. The basic contours of the resulting account of the final reconciliation would look something like this.

First, the reconciling event would not apply to some crimes of some people but to any (social) sin of any person; it would include all injustices, deceptions, and violences, whether minuscule or grand, whether committed intentionally or not, and whether the perpetrators were conscious of them or not.[41] As a result, a clear division between the group of perpetrators and the group of victims would be broken,[42] yet without blunting a sharp condemnation of the evil committed. Second, the judge as the third party would not simply define and set the process in motion but would, in the precise function of a judge who suffered the victim's fate and was judged in the perpetrator's place, be at the very center of their reconciliation. Third, reconciliation between perpetrator and victim would be de-coupled from its necessary relation to the pain of the perpetrator, except for the pain of remorse; healing would be ascribed to the power of God's Spirit working through the display of truth and grace. Fourth, transformation of both perpetrators and victims would be affirmed; perpetrators would be liberated from their sin and (likely?) attempts at self-justification, and victims from their pain and (possible?) bitterness and vindictiveness.

So far have I made two circles of arguments for the final social reconciliation as an aspect of the eschatological transition wrought by God's Spirit. The first centered on a discrepancy between the traditional accounts of the eschatological transition (the last judgment and the resurrection of the dead) and the terminal point to which the transition was leading (the world of love). The second circle consisted of a critical engagement with Socrates' vision how curable perpetrators are saved from the pains of Tartarus. So far my aim was to create a circumference of plausibility for strictly theological arguments. Much will depend on whether *these* arguments, to which I now turn, are persuasive (or, if not, on whether persuasive ones can be found).

Social Reconciliation at the End

In the following I will progress from the background arguments, taken from anthropology and hamartiology, to the central arguments, taken from soteriology and above all eschatology. The constraints of this essay require me to move faster through the territory I need to cover than I would want. I will stop to highlight and argue for only what is absolutely essential for my purposes without situating my claims within an overarching account of the doctrines in question.

The central anthropological question in relation to the final reconciliation concerns the construction of human identity.[43] If identity—not personhood, which I take to be exclusively a gift of God[44]—is constructed in a social process, then one should expect that the transition to a world of love will not circumvent social process. This holds true whether one understands the person as "a structure of response sedimented from a significant history of communication"[45] or if one distinguishes clearly between the "pattern of sedimented communication" and the "organizer of the pattern", as I prefer. In either case, personal *identity* is shaped by how others relate to persons and by how persons internalize others' relation to them; by how persons actively relate to others and by what they do to themselves and with themselves, including their material practices, in relation to others; by narrower and wider public resonances they help shape and are in turn marked by them,[46] by identification with and divergence from others' investments in specific cultural forms broadly conceived, ranging from language and religion to political and economic institutions and activities.[47] The specific identity of persons results from conscious or unconscious complex relations to culturally situated others. Whatever the concrete shape of these relations turns out to be, selfhood, as Paul Ricoeur has argued in *Oneself as Another*, "implies otherness to such an intimate degree that one cannot be thought of without the other".[48] Significantly, given the temporal character of human lives, the shaping of the self in interaction with others has a diachronic and not only a synchronic dimension. Remembered and suppressed past interrelations with others and anticipated future interrelations all flow into one's ever-changing present identity.[49]

The social construction of personal identity correlates with the essentially social character of personal sin.[50] As the preceding anthropological reflection suggests, it would be a mistake to oppose abstractly social sin and personal sin.[51] Personal sin is always socially mediated (though not socially *caused!*); and social sin—evil enshrined in societal institutions, cultural and religious symbols, ideologies which legitimize these institutions and symbols, and collective decisions grounded in ideologies[52]—is as sin always personally embodied (though not reducible to a specific person's attitudes and actions). Though all sin is, by definition, sin against God, most sin is committed in a multi-directional and multi-layered interaction between people, an interaction with both diachronic and synchronic dimensions. It manifests itself, for instance, as "the monstrous injustice of generational succession", to use Oliver O'Donovan's formulation in *The Desire of the Nations*,[53] in which later generations both benefit from the sufferings of earlier ones and suffer the consequences of their misdeeds. Or it takes the form of conflict between persons and communities in which violence, injustice, and deception are the order of the day, and in which the weak suffer at the hands of the strong and the rage of today's victims gives birth to tomorrow's perpetrators. Moreover, sin itself creates a bond between persons which goes beyond the bond that their interrelations in and of themselves create. Evil committed and suffered both severs relationships and weaves a thick network of perverted ties that keep victims and perpetrators returning to each other—in thought, in person, in progeny, or in succeeding generations—to commit new offences in an attempt to rectify the old ones. This partly explains the power of sin, which is located neither simply inside nor simply outside of the person but both in a person and in social relations.

Insofar as a person is involved in a history of sin, the socially constructed identity of a person is a socially constructed identity of a sinner-and-sinned-against-one, an identity that is also temporarily structured through complex interrelations of remembered or suppressed pasts, experienced presents, and anticipated futures. If this is true of the identity of a person in a world of sin, then we can expect the transformation and healing of persons to be socially mediated (an expectation, which, as I will argue shortly, leaves a wide range of possibilities for construing the relation between divine and human action in the process of transformation). And in fact salvation according to Christian soteriology is fundamentally a social reality, whatever else it is in addition to that. Communion with the Triune God is at the same time communion with all those who have entrusted themselves in faith to that same God. As Eberhard Jüngel argues in *God as the Mystery of the World*, "at the very same time that I discover this new fellowship with God" I also discover others "to be my neighbors, who belong to that same fellowship".[54] Reconciliation with one's estranged neighbors is integral to the reconciliation with God. The divine embrace of both the victim and the perpetrator has, in a sense, not come to completion without their own embrace. But how can people who have transgressed against each other embrace? How can their common past be redeemed so that they can have a new future? If one assumes personal continuity between a person as a sinner and as a recipient of grace and affirms the irreversibility of life, creation of a completely new past is out of the question. Rather, their past must be redeemed through reconciliation between them. Dealing adequately with sins suffered and committed is *a social process*, involving individual persons and their fellow human beings.

As an illustration of the essential sociality of the healing process, consider the story Simon Wiesenthal tells in *The Sunflower* about receiving a deathbed confession from an SS soldier for killing a Jewish family trying to flee a building to which the Nazis had set fire.[55] Plagued by guilt, the perpetrator wants forgiveness from a Jew. Though deeply moved, Wiesenthal leaves him without a word, partly on the grounds that victims alone can forgive the crimes done against them. The perpetrator's request and Wiesenthal's refusal are instructive. The request comes out of a painful awareness that the remorseful perpetrator cannot deal with the evil he committed on his own. He needs his victim's mercy so much that, in the absence of his victim, he feels compelled to search for a substitute. Wiesenthal's refusal to show mercy stems from the correct insight that a third party cannot forgive and mend the relations between the offender and the offended.[56] But what about God? Should not God's forgiveness be all that is needed? Though God, being God and therefore not a mere "third party", can forgive, divine forgiveness of sinners would be falsely understood if it was thought that it could substitute for the victim's giving and the perpetrator's receiving of forgiveness. If divine forgiveness could substitute for inter-human forgiveness, it would, in Matthean terms, make it unnecessary for persons who remembered that their brother or sister had something against them to go and be reconciled to them before offering their gifts "at the altar" (Matt. 5:23–24).

If, because of the character of human beings and their sin, salvation includes social reconciliation, then the eschatological consummation of salvation should include it too. The inference gains even more plausibility if we keep in mind that, unlike, for instance, the Marxian vision of a communist revolution, the eschatological consummation is not simply about the future—about the creation of a new future. It is rather about the future of yesterday, today, and tomorrow, about the future of all lived times.[57] If the past suffused with enmity is to be redeemed, then social reconciliation of those who died unreconciled will be included in the eschatological transition. In addition to this more formal eschatological argument, good arguments for the final social reconciliation are inscribed in the three central features of the last judgment. The last judgment is an enactment of God's grace (as well as of justice), it is a social event, and it aims at its own personal appropriation. I will briefly describe each of these features of the last judgment, but expound more extensively its neglected interpersonal character.

First, on the Last Day a judgment of *grace* will be passed—again, grace understood not as excluding justice but as affirming justice in the very act of transcending it. The judge will be none other than the Christ, who died in the place of those who sinned and suffered the fate of those who were sinned against. Since "the judgment day is *his* day (Phil. 1:6; 1 Cor. 1:8)" and "the seat of judgment is *his* seat (2 Cor. 5:10)", the last judgment "cannot, under any circumstances, be perceived as interfering with or rendering problematic the judgment which leads to the justification" of the ungodly,[58] rightly argues Eberhard Jüngel, along with a chorus of other contemporary theologians. It would be a mistake, however, to think of the judgment of grace as a lenient judgment. To the contrary. "There is no more severe judgment possible than that which is effected by grace and measures everything against grace."[59] On the judgment day all persons' sins will be narrated in their full magnitude. But since this will happen in the context of grace,[60] they will be freed from guilt and transformed by that same Christ who has already become their "righteousness and sanctification" (1 Cor. 1:30).

Second, in Old Testament eschatological prophecies judgment is a *social* event. The Lord will judge between Israel and its oppressive leaders (Ezek. 34:17, 20, 22) and "between many peoples" and "strong nations far away" (Micah 4:1–3; Isa. 2:4). Behind these prophecies lie a notion of judgment, fixed in the legal formula, "Let Yahweh judge between you and me",[61] whose goal is "the restoration of *shalom* which prevailed prior to the prevailing strife or dispute".[62] Especially with *shalom* as its goal, judgment cannot simply take place in relation to each of the parties for themselves with the consequence of establishing their guilt or innocence and punishing or rewarding them, but *must also take place with respect to both together with the consequence of redefining their relationship.*

Significantly, the expectation of a "judgment between" seems to be one of the Old Testament sources of the belief in an afterlife, which emerges somewhat tenuously on the margins of its traditions.[63] Arguably, a major reason why this expectation inches itself to the surface in the Old Testament has to do with the experience of injustice (see Ps. 73).[64] To describe the nature of the injustice in question it is insufficient simply to point to innocent suffering. The social dimension of this suffering needs to be brought clearly into focus. The injustice does not consist only in the fact that the "upright" suffer rather than enjoy good fortunes; more precisely, it consists in the fact that they suffer *whereas* the "arrogant" prosper. In Psalm 73, the statement: "[A]fterward you will receive me to glory", is the response to *this social problem* (Ps. 73:24; cf. Job 21:7–15; Jer. 12:1–4).[65] The expectation of enduring communion with God for the upright (Ps. 73:23–28) is meant not simply as a recompense of sorts for suffering, but also as a response to the injustice that their suffering represents when set over against the good fortunes of the arrogant, especially their oppressors.[66] The emergent notion of the final judgment in the Old Testament concerns relations *between* people.

A compelling account of the last judgment's social character—indeed, of its political and world-historical character—can be found in the thought of Jonathan Edwards. Starting with the presupposition that all human beings through all generations "have moral concerns one with another" because they are "linked together", Edwards argued for the last judgment as a universal public event. The "causes and controversies" between individual persons (such as between a parent and a child), between rulers of nations (such as between Roman emperors and the kings they conquered), between peoples (such as between "the Spaniards and Portuguese" and "all the nations of South America"), indeed between whole generations (even those which lived "a thousand years" apart) will be settled by God as the lawgiver and judge.[67] As the frequency of the preposition "between" in Edwards' text attests, the last judgment is fundamentally a social event. Given the interconnections between human beings, all have a case against all and each has to receive justice with respect to all.

Third, as a transition to the world of perfect love, the last judgment is unthinkable without its *appropriation* by persons on whom it is effected. The divine judgment will reach its goal when, by the power of the Spirit,[68] all eschew attempts at self-justification, acknowledge their own sin in its full magnitude, experience liberation from guilt and the power of sin, and, finally, when each recognizes that all others have done precisely that—given up on self-justification, acknowledged their sin, and experienced liberation. Having recognized that others have changed—that they have been given their true identity by being freed from sin—one will no longer condemn others but offer them the grace of forgiveness.[69] When that happens, each will see himself or herself and all others in relation to himself or herself as does Christ, the judge who was judged in their place and suffered their fate.[70]

In a kind of reversal of the parable of the unforgiving servant at which the parable itself aims (Matt. 18:23–35), at the Last Day the grace truly received by the power of the Spirit will translate itself into an unreserved and irrevocable gift of grace to others and, since one is always both a victim and a perpetrator, the reception of grace by others. Indeed, to accept God's judgment of grace fully means to offer grace to offenders and to receive grace from the offended. For those, however, for whom the judgment day does not become the day of giving and receiving grace, it will become a day of wrath leading to a hellish world of indifference and hate.[71] Seeking to justify themselves as Christ the judge reveals the truth about their lives, they will, in Matthean terms, seize their debtors "by the throat", demand payment, and, since it will not be forthcoming, condemn them "into the prison" until they do pay (Matt. 18:30). They will have thereby shown themselves as not having received divine grace and will therefore be "handed over" by God "to be tortured" until they pay their "entire debt" (Matt. 18:34). To refuse to show grace to the offender and to receive grace from the offended, is to have rejected God's judgment of grace.

With the personal appropriation of the divine judgment of grace between people we have entered the space in which the last judgment is becoming the social event of the final reconciliation. But just as forgiveness of even those offenses for which true repentance was made is not yet reconciliation between enemies, so appropriation of the divine judgment is not yet social reconciliation. Reconciliation has not yet taken place when individuals have changed in relation to the transgression inflicted and suffered. Though it is indispensable for each to assent to God's truthful and just resolution of all disputes and give to others and receive from others the same grace of forgiveness contained in Christ's judgment of grace, still more is required to enter the world of love. For if nothing more than all this happened, each could still go his or her own way, fully satisfied that justice has been served and mercy shown. Reconciliation will not have taken place until one has *moved toward one's former enemies* and *embraced them* as belonging to the same communion of love.[72] With that mutual embrace, made possible by the Spirit of communion and grounded in God's embrace of sinful humanity on the cross, all will have stepped into a world in which each enjoys the other in the communion of the Triune God and therefore all take part in the dance of love freely given and freely received.

Reconciliation—Divine Act and Human Agency

An important test-case for the plausibility of my proposal concerns its compatibility with the affirmations that human beings were reconciled with one another in Christ and that the subject of the eschatological transition is God rather than human beings. The main function of these affirmations in relation to the eschatological transition is to give certainty to its outcome. Everything has already been accomplished *de jure* in Christ (to use Karl Barth's favorite way of putting it), and whatever still remains to be done so that it would be realized also *de facto*, is an unfailing divine work. The thesis about the final social reconciliation seems to introduce uncertainty because it presupposes limited and fallible human beings as participants, and that not only in relation to God but in relation to one another. I will argue in the following that this is in fact not the case. In order to develop my argument adequately, I would need to offer a positive account of the relation between the divine act and human agency in the eschatological transition. Since such an account is well beyond the scope of this essay, I will address the issue by indicating minimal requirements with respect to human participation which need to be satisfied for the proposal to work. The advantage of this procedure is that, if successful, it will open a wide space for the proposal's reception by making plausible its compatibility with the most radical assertion that the work of salvation is finished and that the will's turning to God and holding onto God is itself God's work.

One can object to my thesis about the final social reconciliation by arguing that inter-human reconciliation is already included in the *finished* work of Christ. Do we not read in Ephesians that Christ "has made both groups [the Jews and the Gentiles] into one" and that he has abolished the law so as to create "in himself one new humanity" and "reconcile both groups in one body through the cross" (2:14–16)? What room could there be for the eschatological reconciliation, given that one new and fully reconciled humanity is already created in Christ? We can imagine the same objection from the perspective of Karl Barth's powerful re-statement of the doctrine of reconciliation —or at least from a particular reading of it. From the side of humanity, reconciliation in Christ, whose history is identical with the history of humanity, means that "we are lifted up, that we are awakened to our own truest being as life and act, that we are set in motion by the fact that in that one man God has made Himself our peacemaker and the giver and gift of our salvation".[73] What other reconciling activity between human beings would need to happen at the end of history that has not already happened in its middle—indeed, before its beginning—by the inclusion of all humanity into the history of Jesus Christ?

Does the objection stand, however? Consider again the epistle to the Ephesians. It resists a reading that would render reconciling activity of flesh-and-blood people superfluous. One of its main purposes, if not the main purpose, was in fact to encourage the recipients to "make every effort to maintain the unity of the Spirit in the bond of peace" (4:3). As to Karl Barth's doctrine of reconciliation, readings of his thought according to which the force of divine action renders human participation superfluous have proven implausible.[74] The very text I quoted above continues, "What remains to us of life and activity in the face of this actualization of His redemptive will by Himself ... is not for us a passive presence as spectators, but our true and highest activation."[75] Barth's affirmation of the reality of the human acting subject is robust. He is only "unwilling so to emphasise" this reality "that it becomes detached from its gracious origin and its sustaining energy in the act of God".[76]

Now, one may not wish to state together with Barth that the history of God's act of reconciling us to himself simply "*is* our true history",[77] without immediately pointing to the obvious ways in which our history has yet to be transformed. One may find, for instance, the implication implausible that a Serb and a Kosovar—to take an example from the war that is raging as I write these lines—now deeply at odds with each other, *have been reconciled to each other* even before they existed, let alone before they had any quarrel with one another. I certainly do. But even if one advocated as radical a position as Barth's, the thesis about the final social reconciliation can stand. Given his stress on sanctification and vocation, on "the resurrection and the Holy Spirit in which the outgoing, self-realizing character of reconciliation is articulated",[78] Barth cannot let reconciliation simply float above people, disconnected from their concrete relationships. No doctrine of reconciliation can be adequate which denies that an inter-human reconciliation ought to happen that is "in some non-trivial sense ... the very own act of the persons in need of mutual reconciliation".[79] If so, then the idea that human beings have been reconciled in Christ to God and one another does not render the notion of the final social reconciliation problematic. It leaves room for an understanding of the final social reconciliation as the Holy Spirit's perfecting of the inter-human reconciliation which God has accomplished in Christ and in which human beings have been involved all along in response to God's call.

Since reconciliation between two parties requires their involvement because it cannot take place "above" them, the notion of the final social reconciliation leads inevitably to the question of agency. If they are involved, how is their involvement related to divine involvement, which in the tradition so unmistakably and universally dominates the scene of the last judgment? Commenting on the character of the eschatological consummation, Oswald Bayer draws on the prophetic, dominical, and apostolic metaphor of the eschatological feast, and claims:

> Solche Gemeinschaft, in der Trennung, Vereinsamung und Isolierung ueberwunden sind, ist nicht erarbeitet und erworben, nicht von der Welt-geschichte erwirtschaftet, sondern von Gott gewaehrt, geschenkt, von ihm zuvor "bereitet", wie es zugespitzt in der Erzaehlung vom Grossen Weltgericht heisst (Mt. 25:34).[80]

The basic contrast Bayer draws is a familiar one. It is between divine action and human "work". And certainly, if it is anywhere appropriate to stress divine action, it is so with respect to the final consummation. Does the contrast, however, call into question the thesis about the final social reconciliation? It would, if it sufficed simply, negatively, to draw the contrast between divine action and human agency. But it does not suffice. Take, for example, the metaphor of the eschatological feast, on which Bayer's comments lean. If the feast were just about having one's hunger sated, then it would do to highlight only the contrast. If the feast is about celebrating, however, then it is essential also to explore how divine action is positively related to humans coming to enjoy one another's presence. Whatever one's position on synergism may be,[81] it should be uncontested that human beings are not simply passive objects—like blocks of wood—of God's action. That "the sons of the kingdom" are "not preparing the kingdom" but "are being prepared" for the kingdom does not in any way, following Luther,[82] undermine the claim that God *"does not work in us without us"*.[83] Indeed, no stronger claim regarding the relation between divine action and human agency vis-à-vis final social reconciliation can be found.

Just as God's action of preparing the children for the kingdom is indisputable, so God's "not-acting-in-them-without-them" is indispensable. Contrary to Bayer, the communion cannot be created "before" the actual reconciliation of enemies who belong to the communion. True, in Matthew's account of the judgment of the nations, Jesus does say to those on his right, "Come, you that are blessed by my Father, inherit the kingdom *prepared* for you from the foundation of the world" (25:34). But the kingdom here refers here to the "space and time" of the communion and the conditions for the communion, not to the communion of the kingdom's denizens itself. For Jesus refers to something that is not constituted by the entry of persons, whereas the communion is by definition constituted by it. God has prepared "the kingdom" without any human participation, but human beings do participate in the entry into the kingdom. "Enter!" they are told by the judge. Though Matthew does not have the final reconciliation in view, my argument in this essay is that the final reconciliation is an essential dimension of this entry.

Let me conclude by commenting briefly on the import of my endeavor here. Formally, I have attempted to suggest a better fit between the account of the eschatological transition on the one hand and the Christian belief that "heaven" is a world of love as well as the beliefs about the construction of identity, the character of human sin, and the shape of salvation on the other hand. If persuasive, the thesis about the final social reconciliation is a modest contribution to greater consistency among Christian doctrines.

Materially, I have highlighted three important and interrelated aspects of the eschatological transition. First, over against an almost exclusive concentration on individual human beings and their destinies in most accounts of the eschatological transition, I have argued that we should also take seriously human beings as social beings, whose personal identities are inextricably bound up with their near and distant neighbors. Second, I have endeavored to move away from the dominance of justice as desert in the eschatological transformation.[84] Concern for justice is absolutely indispensable, of course, but it is salutary and theologically adequate only as a constituent part of the more overarching notion of grace. I take this to be a basic insight about social relations inscribed in the logic of God's treatment of sinful humanity as evident in the doctrines of atonement, of salvation, and of the last judgment. Third, I have attempted to thematize more clearly the character and import of human participation as an inter-human activity within the overarching account of the eschatological transition accomplished by the power of the Spirit.

The combined emphasis on divine grace as the defining origin and sustaining power of the whole process, on human participation as a fruit and indispensable medium of that grace that transforms sinful persons and their relationships, and on the community of love in the Triune God as the goal of the process explains the introduction of the category "social reconciliation" into the transition from a world of sin to the world of perfect love. The final reconciliation is the eschatological side of the vision of social transformation contained in the movement of the Triune God toward sinful humanity to take them up into the circle of divine communal love.[85] The notion of the final reconciliation strengthens that vision and thus shapes social practices.[86]

NOTES

1   The title of Jonathan Edwards' fifteenth sermon in the collection *Charity and Its Fruits* is "Heaven is a World of Love" (*The Works of Jonathan Edwards*, John E. Smith [ed], [New Haven, CT: Yale University Press, 1957–], VIII, pp. 366–397). Cf. Amy Plantinga Pauw, " 'Heaven is a World of Love': Edwards on Heaven and the Trinity", *Calvin Theological Journal*, 30 (1995), pp. 392–401.

2   Professor Jürgen Moltmann has drawn my attention to this custom. In the printed burial service for the prominent Tübingen New Testament scholar, Professor Ernst Käsemann, we read: "Wir denken vor Gott in der Stille: an den Verstorbenen, an jene, die eng mit Ernst Käsemann verbunden waren, an jene, denen Ernst Käsemann nicht gerecht geworden ist, an jene, die ihm nicht gerecht geworden sind, and jene, die darauf warten, dass wir uns lossagen von den Herrschern, die ueber uns herrschen ..." (*Transparent* 52/98, p. 19).

3   See Brian E. Daley, *The Hope of the Early Church: A Handbook of Patristic Eschatology* (Cambridge: Cambridge University Press, 1991), pp. 131ff.

4   On the social character of Augustine's eschatology see Henri Irenée Marrou, *The Resurrection and Saint Augustine's Theology of Human Values*, trans. M. Consolata (Villanova, PA: Villanova University Press, 1966), p. 33.

5   Augustine, *The City of God*, in Whitney J. Oates (ed), *Basic Writings of Saint Augustine* (New York, NY: Random House, 1948), xix, 17.

6   Ibid., xix, 18.

7   Ibid., xx, 1–3.

8   Ibid., xx, 22.

9   Ibid., xx, 1.

10 In his critical engagement with the doctrine of the last judgment, Friedrich Schleiermacher rightly noted that the notion of the last judgment as separation of the believing and unbelieving requires as supplement a notion of the "inner separation" of believers from "those elements of sinfulness and carnality which still cling to them". Such inner separation, he claimed, "would simply be completed sanctification" (*The Christian Faith*, trans. H. R. Mackintosh and J. S. Stewart [Philadelphia, PA: Fortress Press, 1976], p. 714 [#162]).

11 See Stanislaw Budzik, *Doctor pacis. Theologie des Friedens bei Augustinus* (Innsbruck: Tyrolia Verlag, 1988), pp. 310–322.

12 See John Polkinghorne, *The Faith of a Physicist: Reflections of a Bottom-up Thinker* (Princeton, NJ: Princeton University Press, 1994), p. 167; Jürgen Moltmann, *The Coming of God: Christian Eschatology*, trans. Margaret Kohl (Philadelphia, PA: Fortress Press, 1996), p. 265.

13 Cf. Augustine, xx, 9.

14 Augustine's comments on purgatorial punishments (ibid., xx, 25; xxi, 24) may leave space open for this second option. The later developments of the doctrine of purgatory thematize only the individual's standing before God—and in relation to *that* problem they also speak of the relation of the pilgrim church and the church triumphant to the church suffering. Individuals' standing before one another—the history of their mutual sin and the need for reconciliation—is dealt with at the threshold of purgatory. Though the souls in purgatory "love each other with a supernatural charity which has its source in God", which makes purgatory "a region of that perfect fraternal charity, so easily missed on earth", there nonetheless is "scarcely a soul in Purgatory that is not expiating some faults against charity"

(Martin Jugie, *Purgatory and the Means to Avoid it*, trans. M. G. Carroll [Westminster, MD: The Newman Press, 1949], p. 41). But given that they perfectly love each other nothing needs to change in their relationship while in purgatory; since they are in purgatory, they are not in need of reconciliation. If former enemies, they are rather eager "to show the sincerity of their reconciliation" (p. 42).

15　See Ole Modalsli, "Luther über die Letzten Dinge", in Helmar Junghans (ed), *Leben und Werk Martin Luthers von 1526 bis 1546: Festgabe zu seinem 500. Geburtstag* (Göttingen: Vandenhoeck & Ruprecht, 1983), I, pp. 334–344.

16　Martin Luther, "Sermon on Luke 7:11–17", in Eugene F. A. Klug (ed and trans.), *Sermons of Martin Luther: The House Postils* (Grand Rapids, MI: Baker Books, 1996), iii, p. 34.

17　Martin Luther, *Luther's Works*, Jaroslav Pelikan (ed), trans. M. H. Bertram (Saint Louis, MO: Concordia Publishing House, 1959), xxiii, p. 58.

18　For a powerful contemporary restatement of this position see, for instance, Eberhard Jüngel, "The Last Judgment as an Act of Grace", *Louvain Studies* 15 (1990), pp. 389–405.

19　Schleiermacher, p. 714.

20　The refusal to *receive* "justification" from the other entails a refusal to see oneself as the other sees one and to accept the way the other relates to one. It constitutes therefore refusal of communion, at least until perspectives have been readjusted. This anthropological phenomenon makes plain why soteriologically unbelief, understood as refusal to receive divine justification, constitutes a rejection of communion between God and oneself, especially since, unlike judgments of our human neighbors, God's judgment of us entailed in the offer of justification is, by definition, infallible.

21　For a discussion of the eschatological consummation as the work of the Spirit see Wolfhart Pannenberg, *Systematic Theology*, trans. Geoffrey W. Bromiley (Grand Rapids, MI: Wm. B. Eerdmans Publishing Company, 1998), vol. 3, pp. 550–555.

22　See Friedrich Mildenberger, *Biblische Dogmatik. Eine Biblische Theologie in dogmatischer Perspektive. Band 3. Theologie als Oekonomie* (Stuttgart: Kohlhammer, 1993), pp. 279–280.

23　Gregory of Nyssa writes: "Wrapped up as it is in material and earthly attachments, it [the soul] struggles and is stretched, as God draws His own to Himself. What is alien to God has to be scraped off forcibly because it has somehow grown onto the soul" (*On the Soul and the Resurrection*, trans. Catharine P. Roth [Crestwood, NY: St. Vladimir's Seminary Press, 1993], p. 84).

24　Pannenberg, p. 607.

25　After I had already argued for the final reconciliation in "Sin, Death, and the Life of the World to Come" (prepared for the consultation on "Eschatology and Science" at the Center of Theological Inquiry, Princeton), I came across an article by Josef Niewiadomski, at the end of which he briefly suggests something like "the final reconciliation" as an inter-human process. He imagines the last judgment as an event in which all victims and all perpetrators will face each other and in which the evil suffered and inflicted will be fully manifest to each person. Were it not for God's immeasurable goodness and unlimited willingness to forgive, such an encounter of victims and perpetrators would amount to a day of wrath in which all, prone as human beings are to self-justification and accusation of others, would condemn each other to hell. "Each would insist on his or her own status as a victim, each would demand retaliation and each would seek to place on others the punishment that he or she ought to receive" ("Hoffnung im Gericht. Soteriologische Impulse für eine dogmatische Eschatologie", *Zeitschrift für katholische Theologie*, 114 [1992], pp. 113–126, p. 126). Yet, faced with the radical grace of divine forgiveness, "hardly anyone will withhold forgiveness and continue to insist anachronistically upon his or her own right and revenge" (p. 126). The judgment day will therefore be a day on which divine mercy toward humanity will elicit individuals' mercy toward each other. As will become clear at the end of my essay, my proposal differs from Niewiadomski's in two major respects. First, he does not ground the appropriation of the final judgment of grace pneumatologically, and, second, he fails to make the critical step from forgiveness to reconciliation.

26　Plato, *Phaedo*, 114d, in *Dialogues of Plato*, trans. B. Jowett (Oxford: Clarendon Press, 1875).

27　Ibid., 61d.

28　See David A. White, *Myth and Metaphysics in Plato's Phaedo* (Selinsgrove, PA: Susquehanna University Press, 1989).

29 So Kenneth Dorter, *Plato's Phaedo: An Interpretation* (Toronto: University of Toronto Press, 1982).

30 Plato, 112a.

31 Cf. ibid., 90a.

32 Ibid., 113c–114c.

33 Some critiques of Socrates' account of the curable souls' redemption rest on a misreading, however. Kenneth Dorter, for instance, objects that it presupposes that the victims must be in the Acherusian lake (in whose proximity flow the rivers Cocytus and Pyriphlegethon from which the perpetrators call upon the victims) and that therefore those perpetrators cannot be forgiven whose victims are not in the lake because they have lived a virtuous life or have purified themselves by philosophy, thus standing in no need of purification (Dorter, p. 172). But the reason why the perpetrators call for the victims in the vicinity of the Acherusian lake need not lie in the fact that the victims are in the lake, but that *the perpetrators need to go into the lake* (to be further purified and then "be born as animals" [Plato, 113a]) if the victims have mercy on them. They call upon the victims, Plato says, "to have pity on them, and to be kind to them, *and let them come out into the lake*". Even more problematic is the suggestion of Renna Burger, predicated on the same misconception. She argues that "Socrates, who may never have to pay a penalty for injustice in the Acherusian lake, would thus condemn to eternal punishment in Hades the Athenian demos, who condemned him to death in one day and then lived to repent it" (*The Phaedo: A Platonic Labyrinth* [New Haven, CT: Yale University Press, 1982, p. 202; similarly Peter J. Ahrensdorf, *The Death of Socrates and the Life of Philosophy: An Interpretation of Plato's Phaedo* [Albany, NY: State University of New York Press, 1995], p. 192). But Burger fails to note that, according to the myth, the condemnation of Socrates does not qualify as a remediable crime in the first place because involuntariness is an essential feature of such crimes, and therefore does not apply to the case at all.

34 White, p. 261.

35 The unpardonable sin—blasphemy against the Holy Spirit—was, following Augustine, taken to refer to the final impenitence, not to an act of sin, however heinous. "This blasphemy", argued Augustine, "cannot be detected in anyone ... as long as they are still in this life"; and except for "an impenitent heart against the Holy Spirit, by which sins are cancelled in the Church", he claimed, "all [other] sins are forgiven" (Sermon 71,21, in *The Works of Saint Augustine. Sermons III*, trans. Edmund Hill, ed. John E. Rotelle [Brooklyn, NY: New City Press, 1991], pp. 259f.).

36 For a restatement of the doctrine of purgatory at whose core is "the pain of self-discovery", see David Brown, "No Heaven Without Purgatory", *Religious Studies* 21 (1985), pp. 447–456.

37 See Miroslav Volf, "The Social Meaning of Reconciliation" (forthcoming).

38 Plato, 113a.

39 Dorter, p. 173. Dorter misreads Socrates when he ridicules his position in the following way: "Thus the more spiteful the victim the longer the punishment, in which case one seems best advised to seek out benevolent people as one's victims" (p. 173). The logic is impeccable, the only trouble being that a condition for a crime to qualify as remediable is precisely that it was not premeditated!

40 Plato, *Laws*, 865ff.

41 *All* (social) sins are offenses against others and therefore make those who commit them into perpetrators and those who suffer them into victims. Such a notion of "perpetrators and victims", which is mandated by Christian theology, is at odds with the dominant contemporary construals of perpetrators and victims. It is an important aspect of the public responsibility of Christian theology to problematize these construals.

42 There is no reason to think that in Socrates' account of the post-mortem destiny of curable souls a victim could not also be a perpetrator. However, the principle seems to hold: the greater the sin required to qualify one as a perpetrator, the clearer the division between perpetrators and the rest. A theologically adequate doctrine of sin, whose one characteristic is not to let any evil—not even an evil thought—remain uncondemned, works against a clear division of humanity into perpetrators and victims.

43 For recent theological accounts of the construction of identity see Ingolf U. Dalferth and Eberhard Jüngel, "Person and Gottebenbildlichkeit", in F. Boeckle *et al.* (eds), *Christlicher Glaube in moderner Gesellschaft* (Freiburg: Herder, 1981), xxiv, pp. 57–99;

Wolfhart Pannenberg, *Anthropology in Theological Perspective*, trans. M. J. O'Connell (Edinburgh: T&T Clark, 1985).

44   See Miroslav Volf, *After Our Likeness: The Church as the Image of the Trinity* (Grand Rapids, MI: Wm. B. Eerdmans Publishing Company, 1998), pp. 181–189.

45   Alistair I. McFadyen, *The Call to Personhood: A Christian Theory of the Individual in Social Relationships* (Cambridge: Cambridge University Press, 1990), p. 114.

46   See Michael Welker, *God the Spirit*, trans. J. F. Hoffmeyer (Minneapolis, MN: Fortress Press, 1994), pp. 312–314. Cf. Niklas Luhmann, *Ecological Communication*, trans. John Bednarz, Jr. (Chicago, IL: University of Chicago Press, 1989), pp. 15–21.

47   Cf. Miroslav Volf, "Cultural Identity and Recognition: On Why the Issue Matters", in Michael Welker (ed), *Brenpunkt Diakonie. Rudolph Weth zum 60. Geburtstag* (Neukirchen-Vlyun: Neukirchener Verlag, 1997), pp. 201–218.

48   Paul Ricoeur, *Oneself as Another*, trans. Kathleen Blamey (Chicago, IL: University of Chicago Press, 1992), p. 3.

49   For a discussion of the temporality of human consciousness in general under the category of "transversality" that reaches forward as well as backward, but from the perspective of a consistent contesting of any notion of a transcendental ego, see Calvin O. Schrag, *The Resources of Rationality: A Response to the Postmodern Challenge* (Bloomington, IN: Indiana University Press, 1992), pp. 148–179.

50   In traditional, broadly Augustinian, hamartiology, sin as *peccatum originale* is also understood as social in the sense of being a socially shared problem on account of the solidarity of the human family. To underscore a different sense in which sin can be seen as social, David Kelsey has introduced the distinction between "social" and "societal", the latter indicating that the social character of sin has to be understood also "in terms of the 'public' realm of actual societies' arrangements of social power" ("Whatever Happened to the Doctrine of Sin?", *Theology Today* 50 (1993), pp. 169–178, pp. 170f.). The distinction is analytically helpful. I have decided not to use the term "societal" to describe important aspects of sin, however, though not for what the term implies about sin but for what it seems to leave out. It fails to take seriously enough cultural and sub-cultural social practices and symbols. When speaking of the social character of sin, I will use the term "social" to refer to both societal arrangements of power and narrower social relations, practices, and symbols.

51   On the interrelation between personal and social sin from the perspective of Catholic theology, see Mark O'Keefe, "Social Sin and Fundamental Option", *Irish Theological Quarterly* 58 (1992), pp. 85–94. Cf. also Siegfried Wiedenhofer, "The Main Forms of Contemporary Theology of Original Sin", *Communio* (US), 18 (1991), pp. 514–529.

52   On these elements of social sin see Gregory Baum, *Religion and Alienation: A Theological Reading of Sociology* (New York, NY: Paulist Press, 1975), pp. 200–203.

53   Oliver O'Donovan, *The Desire of the Nations: Rediscovering the Roots of Political Theology* (Cambridge: Cambridge University Press, 1996), pp. 287–288.

54   Eberhard Jüngel, *God as the Mystery of the World*, trans. D. L. Guder (Grand Rapids, MI: Wm. B. Eerdmans Publishing Company, 1983), p. 354 (slightly revised translation).

55   Simon Wiesenthal, *The Sunflower* (New York, NY: Schocken Books, 1976), pp. 9–99.

56   Together with Milton Konvitz I wish, however, that Wiesenthal had explained his refusal to the perpetrator and then gone on to offer him solace (see Wiesenthal, p. 160; cf. L. Gregory Jones, "Stumped Repentance", *Christianity Today*, October 26, 1998, pp. 94–97). Indeed, I wish he had offered him even forgiveness, though not for the crime against the family killed but for the injury done to Wiesenthal by the crime against the family and the Jewish people. But, of course, it is easier to be wise after the situation than in it.

57   See Miroslav Volf, "After Moltmann: Reflections on the Future of Eschatology", in Richard Bauckham (ed), *God Will be All in All: The Eschatology of Jürgen Moltmann* (Edinburgh: T&T Clark, 1999), pp. 233–257, p. 253.

58   Jüngel, "The Last Judgment", p. 395.

59   Ibid., p. 397.

60   As Hans Urs von Balthasar notes, it is precisely through the look at the one whom one has "pierced" (Rev. 1:7) that one will realize the magnitude of one's sin ("Die goettliche Gerichte in der Apokalypse", *Internationale katholische Zeitschrift Communio*, 14 [1985], pp. 28–34, p. 33). For the cross as the site of recognition of sin's magnitude see Martin

Koehler, *Die Wissenschaft der christlichen Lehre von dem evangelischen Grundartikel aus im Abrisse dargestellt* (Leipzig: A. Diechert, 1893), p. 270: "Am Kreuze Christi ermisst der Gerechtfertigte die Bedeutung der Menschensuende, und erst in und mit dem Verstaendnisse des Heilswerkes vollendet sich die unter dem Gesetze des alten Bundes erwachsende Suendenerkenntnis." For a development of this theme in a broader Christological context see Karl Barth, *Church Dogmatics* IV/1, G. W. Bromiley and T. F. Torrance (eds), (Edinburgh: T&T Clark, 1956), pp. 358–413.

61   See Claus Westermann, *Genesis 12–36: A Commentary*, trans. J. D. Scullion (Minneapolis, MN: Augsburg Press, 1985), p. 241.

62   Temba L. J. Mafico, "Judge, Judging", in *The Anchor Bible Dictionary* vol. III, David Noel Freedman (ed), (New York, NY: Doubleday, 1992), pp. 1104–1106, p. 1105.

63   See Joseph Ratzinger, *Eschatology: Death and Eternal Life*, trans. Michael Waldstein (Washington, DC: The Catholic University of America Press, 1988), pp. 88–90. Cf. Pannenberg, *Systematic Theology*, vol. 3, pp. 563–568.

64   On Psalm 73 in relation to eschatology see Ratzinger, ibid., pp. 88–90. Cf. Diethelm Michel, "Weisheit und Apokalyptik", in A. S. Van der Woude (ed), *The Book of Daniel in the Light of New Findings* (Leuven: Leuven University Press, 1993), pp. 413–434, pp. 420–422. For a view contesting an eschatological reading of the Psalm, see Martin Buber, *On the Bible: Eighteen Studies*, Nahum N. Glatzer (ed), (New York, NY: Schocken Books, 1968), pp. 199–216.

65   In *The City of God* the social problem that the suffering of the upright and the prosperity of the arrogant present is an important backdrop for the discussion of the last judgment. Augustine writes: "For that day is properly called the day of judgment, because in it there shall be no room left for the ignorant questioning why this wicked person is happy and that righteous man unhappy. In that day true and full happiness shall be the lot of none but the good, while deserved and supreme misery shall be the portion of the wicked, and of them only" (xx, 1).

66   This eschatological expectation—assuming that it is such—correlates well with the way the Old Testament poses the problem of theodicy. It concerns primarily social rather than strictly individual evil, such as illness (see Walter Brueggemann, *Theology of the Old Testament: Testimony, Dispute, Advocacy* [Minneapolis, MN: Fortress Press, 1997], pp. 385–399; cf. Walter Brueggemann, "Theodicy in a Social Dimension", *Journal for the Study of the Old Testament*, 33 [1985], pp. 3–25).

67   Jonathan Edwards, entry #1007, from the forthcoming third volume of the "Miscellanies", Amy Plantinga Pauw (ed), in *The Works of Jonathan Edwards*, Harry S. Stout (ed) (New Haven, CT: Yale University Press). Cf. Robert W. Jenson, *America's Theologian: A Recommendation of Jonathan Edwards* (New York, NY: Oxford University Press, 1988), p. 179. It was Robert Jenson who, in a private conversation, originally drew my attention to Edwards' explication of the last judgment as a social event.

68   Behind this formulation, as well as other's that thematize the role of the Holy Spirit in the consummation, lies a transposition into the eschatological mode of the Holy Spirit's role in the appropriation of salvation (cf. Karl Barth, *Church Dogmatics* IV/1, pp. 147ff.), including the role as the one who convicts of sin (cf. John 16:8–11).

69   As the above account of the last judgment's appropriation underscores, the social character of the judgment does not stand in opposition to its personal character. The connection of the two is suggested in Romans 14, where the Apostle Paul writes that "all will stand before the judgment seat of God" and that "each of us will be accountable to God" (Rom. 14:10, 12; cf. 2 Cor. 5:10; Eph. 6:8) (see von Balthasar, ibid., p. 229). The mention of the eschatological judgmental "all" and "each" in a text which condemns judging others may be significant. Between the lines it suggests that the divine judgment of each includes also a judgment about that person's judgment of others and calls implicitly for an alignment of persons' judgment of others with God's judgment of them (see James D. G. Dunn, *Romans 9–16* [Word Bible Commentary, 38b; Dallas, TX: Word Books, 1988], p. 814). Put more generally, the last judgment concerns each person's standing before God, but in such a way that it includes the judgment about what each has done to and suffered from others, and how he or she has integrated relations to others into his or her identity. Hence, to put things personally, when I appropriate God's judgment, I appropriate it as a judgment of me not only in my relation to God but in my multiple and multidirectional relations to all and therefore also as a judgment of all in relation to me.

70 Balthasar introduces the idea of personal appropriation of the judge's perspective when he suggests that the saints will be able to judge "the world" and "angels" (1 Cor. 6:2–3) only when "jeder Einzelne, auch die erwaehnte Heilige, durch seinen Blick auf den Durchgebohrten so gelaeutert ist, dass sein Blick auf die Welt und die Engel sich dem des Menschensohns angeglichen hat" (Hans Urs von Balthasar, "Gericht", *Internationale katholische Zeitschrift 'Communio'* 9 [1980], pp. 227–235, p. 231).

71 Cf. Niewiadomski, p. 126.

72 In the discussion of former enemies entering purgatory, Father Hubert suggests that if the person has not fully forgiven his offenders, on purgatory's threshold "he immediately and completely forgives the injustice. For in purgatory love 'does not brood over an injury' even for an instant. His dispositions toward the offender are those of an unfeigned and tender charity and he prays much for him. If during the purgatory of the onetime injured person, the offender himself goes to purgatory, an immediate and perfect mutual friendship between both is effected under the mighty sway of love. Thus do they imitate their Saviour who forgave his enemies" (*The Mystery of Purgatory* [Chicago, IL: Franciscan Herald Press, 1975], p. 32). In my terminology, this immediate effecting of perfect mutual friendship is reconciliation; the change of individuals' dispositions toward the offender is not, at least not yet.

73 Karl Barth, *Church Dogmatics* IV/1, p. 14.

74 See especially John Webster, *Barth's Ethics of Reconciliation* (Cambridge: Cambridge University Press, 1995); John Webster, *Barth's Moral Theology: Human Action in Barth's Thought* (Edinburgh: T&T Clark, 1998).

75 Barth, ibid., pp. 14f.

76 Webster, *Barth's Ethics*, p. 97—italics added.

77 Barth, *Church Dogmatics* IV/1, p. 547—italics added.

78 Webster, p. 97.

79 George Hunsinger, in a personal communication.

80 Oswald Bayer, "Das Letzte Gericht als religionsphilosophisches Problem", *Neue Zeitschrift für Systematische Theologie* 33 (1991), pp. 199–210, pp. 209f.

81 For Oswald Bayer's explication of Luther's position in contrast to Melanchthon see "Freedom? The Anthropological Concepts in Luther and Melanchthon Compared", *Harvard Theological Review* 91 (1998), pp. 373–378.

82 Martin Luther, *Luther's Works*, Helmut T. Lehmann (ed) (Philadelphia, PA: Fortress Press, 1972), xxxiii, p. 153 (De servo arbitrio).

83 Martin Luther, *Luther's Works*, xxxiii, p. 243. To put my claim in Luther's terms but rather abstractly, in the final reconciliation former enemies act in the precise sense in which human beings must act if God is not simply to act upon them but act in them in such a way as not to act without them.

84 A recent notable eschatology which takes seriously social relations and stresses the primacy of grace in the eschatological transition is Moltmann's *The Coming of God* (see especially pp. 250–255).

85 As the three combined emphases suggest, my reflection on eschatological transition here is part and parcel of specifying the eschatological side of the ecclesial and broader social reflections expressed in my books *After Our Likeness* and *Exclusion and Embrace: A Theological Exploration of Identity, Otherness, and Reconciliation* (Nashville, TN: Abingdon Press, 1996) and in the article " 'The Trinity is Our Social Program': The Doctrine of the Trinity and the Shape of Social Engagement", *Modern Theology* 14 (1998), pp. 403–423.

86 This text was presented as part of the 1999 Laidlaw Lectures series at Knox College, Toronto. I am indebted to Ivica Novakovic, my research assistant, for his extraordinary competence and helpfulness. Professors Robert W. Jenson, George Hunsinger, Patrick D. Miller, Amy Plantinga Pauw, Rusty R. Reno, and Judith M. Gundry-Volf offered helpful comments on a previous draft of the text. I wrote this essay as a Pew scholar and member of the Center for Theological Inquiry, Princeton, New Jersey, where I benefited from the comments of my fellow members.

CHAPTER 7

"WHY DO YOU STAND LOOKING UP TOWARD HEAVEN?" NEW TESTAMENT ESCHATOLOGY AT THE TURN OF THE MILLENNIUM

RICHARD B. HAYS

Besides this, you know what time it is, how it is now the moment for you to wake from sleep. For salvation is nearer to us now than when we became believers; the night is far gone, the day is near.—Rom 13:11–12a

I. Millennial Fever and Backlash

As the twentieth century staggers to its close, the symptoms of millennial fever are on display all around us.

*"This American Life", a radio show on National Public Radio, features an interview with a devout Christian woman who has calculated on the basis of biblical prophecies that Jesus will descend from heaven and bring the world to an end on October 19, 1999.

*A syndicated newspaper story tells of a man who, regarding himself as the Messiah and believing the end to be at hand, would lie on the floor in his workplace and "pretend he was nailed to the cross, frightening co-workers and customers". (The story helpfully goes on to explain that this worker's behavior may be protected by state and federal laws prohibiting religious discrimination in the workplace.)[1]

*An anxious Seventh Day Adventist, having heard a report that the Pope has issued a statement encouraging Christians to observe Sunday as a day of rest, phones my office to ask whether I, as a New Testament scholar, think this might be a harbinger of a new oppressive legal order

Richard B. Hays
The Divinity School, Duke University, Durham, NC 27708, USA

that will mandate Sunday worship and forbid Adventists from observing the sabbath, thus ushering in the reign of Antichrist in the year 2000. *On the Internet, rumors fly that the dreaded Y2K bug will bring down civilization as we know it and perhaps inaugurate the reign of the Antichrist.

These tidbits of news, which could be multiplied many times over, illustrate a widespread popular tendency to believe that human history has reached a desperate state of corruption and that God's final judgment is surely at hand. The current wave of speculation about the year 2000 may be artificially fueled by news media looking for livid curiosities in order to sell news "product"; nonetheless, there is a deep strain of belief in American popular Christianity that the Bible points to an apocalyptic end of all things that is to occur within the current generation. Such beliefs are held not merely by fringe sectarian groups such as the ill-fated Branch Davidians but also by millions of ordinary American Christians who continue to line the pockets of TV evangelists and authors of speculative books on the endtime.[2]

On the other hand, such millennium fever receives its due portion of derision from many sides—not only from comics and pundits who count themselves among the cultured despisers of religion but also from Christian scholars, pastors, and laity who consider themselves too "modern" to countenance such foolishness and who regard apocalyptic ideas as an embarrassing throwback to naive fundamentalism. Thus, in the backlash against millennialist liberalism, many Christians have categorically dismissed the New Testament's apocalyptic imagery. With greater or lesser theological reflection, they have come to think that all ideas about the second coming of Christ are quaint speculations that should be shed by mature, educated believers. The rising millennial fever, with its periodic outbreaks of bizarre or even violent behavior, confirms their worst suspicions and leads to widespread scoffing at the eschatological visions of the New Testament writers. Where this reaction occurs, the already tenuous authority of the New Testament in the church is further undermined.

Yet such a reaction is both hasty and self-defeating, for apocalyptic categories are neither peripheral nor dispensable; they stand at the heart of the gospel of Jesus Christ, as proclaimed and interpreted by the New Testament writers. The resurrection itself is an apocalyptic event, and it can be understood as a saving event for the world only within the framework of the New Testament's dialectical already/not yet eschatology. Thus, Christians who scoff at apocalyptic are sawing off the branch on which they sit—or, to give the metaphor a more biblical turn, tearing out the roots of a tree of which they themselves are the branches. Apocalyptic narrative and apocalyptic expectation are integral to the logic of the gospel.

In order to develop this claim, we must first distinguish between specific millennial speculation and apocalyptic eschatology. The New Testament writers actually discourage the former, while insisting on the latter. The distinction appears clearly in a passage such as Mark 13:24–37, at the end of Jesus' lengthy discourse on the destruction of the temple and the coming of the Son of Man. He tells his disciples that they will see the coming of the Son of Man in power and glory, and that he will gather his elect from the ends of the earth (vv. 24–27). These events are depicted as near and inevitable (vv. 28–31). Then, however, Jesus warns them against trying to predict the date of these occurrences:

> But about that day or hour no one knows, neither the angels in heaven, nor the Son, but only the Father. Beware, keep alert; for you do not know when the time will come (Mark 13:31–32).

Jesus' followers are to stake their lives on the expectation of the coming kingdom of God, when God will restore Israel and establish justice. They are to "stay awake", however, not by gazing up into heaven or frittering away their time in fruitless calculations but by attending to the work that has been assigned to them by their master (Mark 13:34–37). That is the readiness that is required.

When Ernst Käsemann, in reaction against the demythologizing hermeneutic of his teacher Rudolf Bultmann, coined the maxim that "apocalyptic is the mother of Christian theology",[3] he was identifying apocalyptic thought not only as historical background to the development of the New Testament but also as an essential component of the *kerygma*. As I will argue in this essay, Käsemann was exactly correct in this description of the matter. The difficulty that has long plagued the church, however, is how to interpret the New Testament's apocalyptic hope in light of the fact that "all things continue as they were from the beginning of creation" (2 Pet. 3:4b). Does the continuation of history without the *parousia* of the Lord, without the visible righting of all things, disconfirm the gospel? What account can we give, at the dawn of the third millennium since the incarnation, of the future hope that we continue to hold? Is the hope still credible? Or should the gospel proclamation be reformulated to deemphasize eschatological expectation? Should we Christians continue to honor and be instructed by our mother? Or must we regretfully disown her?

II. Three Unsatisfactory Strategies

A cursory survey of some strategies for dealing with this difficult hermeneutical problem shows that some of the solutions historically adopted by Christians are not real solutions: either they fail to resolve the problem or they settle the eschatological problem only by introducing fatal glitches elsewhere in the overall configuration of the theological system. In the latter case, the solution is more damaging than the problem it was designed to remedy. Let us consider three significant but unsatisfactory strategies for coping with the non-fulfillment of apocalyptic expectation.

A. *The Johannine option: eternal life now.* Already within the New Testament itself, we find evidence that Christians were grappling with the problem of reformulating their eschatological expectations, in order to sustain the church into an extended temporal future. The clearest illustration of this development in the New Testament is to be found in the Gospel of John, which took its final form sometime late in the first century, after the death of the Beloved Disciple, the original witness to the community's tradition about Jesus (John 21:23). This gospel is concerned to assure believers that even those who stand removed in time and place from Jesus are nontheless able to be intimately united with him and to share his glory (17:20–26). Consequently, in the Fourth Gospel, future eschatology is emphatically deemphasized and overshadowed by an eschatology claiming eternal life as the *present* possession of those who believe in Jesus. Anyone who believes "has eternal life, and does not come under judgment, but has passed from death to life" (John 5:24; cf. 3:36). Jesus, having ascended to God, *is* the resurrection, and those who are one with him have already entered into his eternal life. That is why Jesus can say paradoxically to Martha, "I am the resurrection and the life. Those who believe in me, even though they die, will live, and everyone who lives and believes in me will never die" (John 11:25–26). In light of this bold claim, there is no need to look forward wistfully to "the resurrection on the last day" (11:24). In Jesus, the resurrection has engulfed the sphere of present temporality, and the future fades into relative insignificance, as does the reality of physical death.

The corollary of this conviction is that, in a real sense, judgment has already taken place whenever anyone hears the gospel and responds either in faith or in unbelief. "Those who believe in him are not condemned; but those who do not believe are condemned already, because they have not believed in the name of the only Son of God" (3:18). Nowhere in John do we hear of a final judgment that will hold any suspense or surprises (unlike, e.g., Matt. 25:31–46). Jesus' entry into the world polarizes humanity into believers and unbelievers, and their eternal destiny is already settled by that polarization, which separates those who love the light from those who love the darkness because their deeds are evil (3:19–21).

To be sure, we do find in John's Gospel a few vestiges of the characteristic early Christian apocalyptic eschatology. For example, Jesus in one place declares that "the hour is coming when all who are in their graves will hear his voice and will come out—those who have done good, to the resurrection of life, and those have done evil, to the resurrection of condemnation" (5:28–29; see also 6:39, 40, 44, 54). Such passages stand out strikingly in a gospel that otherwise proclaims judgment now and eternal life now.

Rudolf Bultmann hypothesized that the few future eschatological passages in John's Gospel were not originally part of the text; they must have been added later by an "ecclesiastical editor" who found John's radical realized eschatology unacceptable.[4] Bultmann's hypothesis is, however, pure speculation. The text of the Fourth Gospel as we have it includes these future-oriented apocalyptic passages as part of the canonical witness of John; there is no manuscript evidence for the existence of any text of John that lacks these passages. Furthermore, the First Letter of John, a later writing in the same Johannine community tradition, takes some care to give prominence to future eschatological themes, urging community members to abide in Jesus "so that when he is revealed we may have confidence and not be put to shame before him at his coming (*parousia*)" (1 John 2:28; cf. 3:2–3, 4:17).[5] Raymond Brown has persuasively argued that 1 John should be read as an attempt to shape and clarify the church's reading of the Fourth Gospel, heading off heretical misreadings and showing how the teaching of the Gospel conforms to the broader church's teachings on eschatology, ethics, the humanity of Jesus, and other topics.[6]

Thus, the realized eschatology that is featured prominently in John's Gospel cannot stand on its own. Taken as a whole, the canonical Johannine texts do not supplant future eschatology with realized eschatology; instead, the future eschatology provides the temporal framework within which the realized eschatology must be understood: i.e., the eternal life that the believer experiences in the present *points forward to* a final consummation in the resurrection at the last day. When John is read this way, his eschatology is formally similar to the dialectical already/not yet eschatology found in Paul, albeit with a much stronger accent on the "already". To the extent that the "not yet" remains essential to John's vision, however, the realized eschatology must be read as poetic hyperbole that fails to resolve the difficulty of non-fulfillment.

On the other hand, if John is read as offering an unqualified eschatology of eternal life in the present, then the problem of non-fulfillment is solved, but at the high price of construing this gospel as incipiently Gnostic, unconcerned about the fate of God's created world, the physical body, and the suffering that we still experience in the present time. All things considered, the Fourth Gospel's depiction of Jesus as "the word made flesh" tells against such a reading; the Jesus who weeps at Lazarus' tomb (11:33–36) can hardly be a Gnostic savior seeking to teach human beings how to transcend time and material existence.

Bultmann, drawing heavily on his reading of John, sought to demythologize apocalyptic eschatology, interpreting it as a primitive symbolic vocabulary that sought to bring to expression a deeper truth about humanity's existential situation before God: we are always confronted at every moment by the demand for decision and the possibility of authentic existence. Thus, in the Fourth Gospel—stripped of the "ecclesiastical editor's" future eschatological passages—Bultmann saw within the New Testament itself a precursor of his own demythologizing program.[7] But this hermeneutical program is subject to some of the same objections enumerated in the previous paragraph: it posits such an exalted anthropology that it fails to account for the limitations and sufferings of human existence as we actually know it, which constantly falls short of the "authenticity" that Bultmann envisioned. Additionally, it has the fatal quasi-Marcionite flaw of producing a trimmed-down text that does away with (Jewish) apocalyptic eschatology in order to suit the requirements of a preconceived anti-apocalyptic program. Any ultimately satisfactory solution to the eschatological problem must attend to the form in which the canonical texts actually present themselves to us; it will not do merely to lop off pieces that fail to conform to our theological agenda.

   B. *The Jesus Seminar: driving a wedge between Jesus and the Gospels.* In his programmatic address at the first meeting of the Jesus Seminar in 1985, Robert Funk pinpointed the New Testament's eschatology as one of the major difficulties that the Seminar must seek to overcome. The New Testament's canonical story of Jesus must be replaced by a new story, Funk proposed, because the New Testament's story of cosmic beginnings and endings has become incredible and therefore useless for modern people who have now seen the heavens through Galileo's telescope. The canonical Jesus is, of course, the Christ of the church's creed, who was raised from the dead and who will come again to judge the world. In order to construct a new Jesus who will be usable and marketable in our day, according to Funk, we must purge the story of such apocalyptic fantasies.[8]

   Funk's initial concern with the untenability of apocalyptic traditions goes a long way towards explaining the Jesus Seminar's subsequent "discovery" of a non-eschatological Jesus. According to *The Five Gospels*, the Seminar's summation of its findings, the real Jesus of history was entirely free of the influence of Jewish apocalyptic thought. Instead, "he had a poetic sense of time in which the future and the present merged, simply melted together, in the intensity of his vision."[9] Consequently, wherever the Gospels portray Jesus as using apocalyptic imagery, such passages are resolutely classified by the Seminar as creations of the early church, those pedestrian blunderers who "reverted, once Jesus was not there to remind them", into their bad old Jewish apocalyptic ways of thinking and retrojected onto Jesus the naive apocalyptic ideas taught by John the Baptist.[10]

   The production of an idealized non-eschatological Jesus is facilitated by the Seminar's highly debatable methodological decision to treat Q and the Gospel of Thomas as the earliest sources for Jesus tradition—with the proviso that the "Q" in question must be an expurgated "early layer" of Q with nearly all the apocalyptic sayings removed! This circular methodology produces just what it was designed to produce: a non-eschatological Jesus, constructed by systematically isolating him from the apocalyptic matrix in which the synoptic evangelists have placed him.

   Marcus Borg, whose own books on Jesus are more careful and much less polemical than Funk's work, has gone so far as to claim that there is now a new consensus among New Testament scholars in support of a non-eschatological Jesus. In his book *Jesus, A New Vision*, he writes, "The majority of scholars no longer thinks that Jesus expected the end of the world in his generation."[11] Although this claim is of doubtful validity, it is certainly true that there have been a number of recent publications seeking to reconstruct Jesus along non-eschatological lines, using methods that, to a greater or lesser extent, parallel Funk's arguments in *The Five Gospels*.[12] The common denominator of these reconstructions is a Jesus who is an itinerant sage, a teacher of subversive wisdom and spirituality, more like a Cynic philosopher than an eschatological prophet. In some cases (Borg, Crossan), Jesus is also credited as the teacher of an alternative vision of social justice.

The difficulties with this portrayal of a non-eschatological Jesus are both historical and theological in character. At the historical level, the method of these revisionist studies drives a wedge between Jesus and the authors who preserved our earliest traditions about him. This is a highly questionable historiographical procedure. As E. P. Sanders has observed, if Jesus was a follower of the apocalyptic prophet John the Baptist and left behind a group of followers whose writings burn with apocalyptic expectation, a heavy burden of proof lies with anyone who contends that Jesus himself did not share in this chain of apocalyptic thinking.[13] Borg's effort to refute this line of argument is unpersuasive.[14] In the present essay I cannot undertake a full discussion of these issues; a recent monograph by Dale C. Allison has undertaken an extended response to Borg and other champions of the "non-eschatological Jesus" thesis.[15]

More to the point of our present concerns is the theological deficiency of this revisionist position. Its advocates—insofar as they have theological concerns—seem to presuppose that only the critically reconstructed Jesus of history is theologically valid and useful.[16] The function of the historical reconstruction is to challenge—or replace—the canonical image of the eschatological Jesus. This solves the problem of eschatological non-fulfillment by dissolving it, eliminating future eschatology from our construal of the gospel. But this strategy leaves us, alas, with no gospel at all. N. T. Wright, in an appreciative critique of Borg, poses the issue tellingly:

> ... is Borg's Jesus really an eschatological figure or does he after all use the language of eschatology to express ... the essentially timeless truth that God is always available to human beings, and requires compassion rather than exclusive and oppressive ways of life? In other words, does Borg's Jesus (like, say, Sanders') suppose that Israel's god was actually *doing* something climactic and unique, in and through which Israel's (and perhaps the world's) story would be brought to some kind of fulfilment?[17]

There is no promise here of a God who will come to rescue humanity from death and injustice, who offers hope beyond the grave. In place of such a hope, we are offered a handful of enigmatic aphorisms that might enable us to reexamine our lives, perhaps even to work for social change. If this strategy has any theological agenda, it is either Pelagian or soft-core pantheist. Either way, the systematic consequences for theology are grave. If our lives and the fate of the human race are in our own hands, we are in deep trouble. As Paul says, if there is no resurrection of the dead, "we are of all people most to be pitied" (1 Cor. 15:19). It is no accident that these new scholarly visions of a non-eschatological Jesus have found their most enthusiastic reception in their natural sociological and theological home: a dwindling but affluent liberal Protestant church in North America seeking some way to reconnect with a kinder, gentler Jesus who will offer them new spiritual stimulation without threatening them with God's final judgment.

The other theological difficulty posed by this strategy is the devaluation of the canon of Scripture. The critique of the canon, in rescuing Jesus from the embarrassments of apocalyptic theology, erodes the foundation of the church's confession. This will not trouble the more aggressive revisionists (e.g., Funk and Mack), whose program has this end explicitly in view. I wonder, however, whether most Christians who find the more benign non-eschatological constructions of Borg and Crossan attractive have fully thought through the consequences of this choice. Given the choice between Mark and Marcus Borg, or between John and John Dominic Crossan as interpreters of dominical eschatology, whom shall we prefer?

C. N. T. Wright: apocalyptic eschatology historicized. Finally, we must offer a brief comment on N. T. Wright's widely-discussed proposals concerning the eschatological sayings of the synoptic gospels. Only the briefest sketch of Wright's ambitious project in *Jesus and the Victory of God* is possible here. Wright treats virtually all of the sayings traditions of the synoptics as authentic material that goes back to Jesus of Nazareth, including the critically contested future Son of Man sayings and the parables that speak of a returning king or master. Thus, he will have no part of any strategy that excises the apocalyptic traditions from our picture of Jesus. Nor is he interested in a strategy of demythologizing that reads these materials as expressions of some timeless truth about God's relationship to the world. Instead, Wright mounts an extended argument that all the apocalyptic sayings in the synoptic tradition were spoken by Jesus as symbolic descriptions of concrete events taking place in and through his own activity in the immediate historical setting of first-century Israel. These sayings employ a symbolic shorthand well recognized in first-century Jewish culture to make claims about the salvation-historical significance of Jesus' own identity and mission.

The "synoptic apocalypse" passages (Mark 13 and parallels) are to be read not as predictions of the end of the world but as prophetic warnings of God's impending judgment and destruction of an unfaithful and unrepentant Jerusalem.[18] The parables of a returning king are not the early church's allegories about a future *parousia*; rather, Jesus told these stories as figurative portrayals of "the return of YHWH to Zion", which Jesus himself symbolically enacted in his climactic journey to Jerusalem.[19] When Jesus declares in his trial before the high priest that "you will see the Son of Man seated at the right hand of the Power and 'coming with the clouds of heaven' " (Mark 14:62), this is not a prophecy of a descent from heaven—a "second coming"—but rather a vision of exaltation and enthronement, as in Daniel 7: Jesus foresees his own final vindication, as Israel's representative and King, at the right hand of God.[20]

The cumulative result of these exegetical proposals is that the apocalyptic prophecies of Jesus are, without remainder, seen to be fulfilled in Jesus' journey to Jerusalem, his death and resurrection, and, finally, the destruction of the Temple by the Romans in 70 C.E. Thus, at least with regard to these sayings, the problem of non-fulfillment is solved, for the world-transforming events to which the sayings point *had already taken place* by the time the gospels were written. Thus, apocalyptic expectation has been both historicized and fulfilled.

It is not possible here to respond in detail to Wright's remarkable comprehensive construal of Jesus' actions, teachings, and intentions. The proposal invites thorough exegetical scrutiny, text by text.[21] For the present I will merely record my response to one key point: with regard to Mark 14:62, Wright has converted me. Daniel 7:13–14 is without question a vision of ascent and enthronement of a human figure representing Israel's vindication and triumph over the kingdoms symbolized by the beasts in the preceding visions.[22] When, in Mark's story, Jesus quotes Daniel to claim this role for himself, the high priest quite understandably judges his words to be blasphemy, because Jesus is foretelling that he will share the divine throne with the Ancient of Days. The parallels in Matt. 26:64 (*"from now on* you will see the Son of Man seated at the right hand of Power ..."*) and Luke 22:69 (*"from now on* the Son of Man will be seated at the right hand of the power of God") are even more clearly to be understood as references to enthronement rather than a future return from heaven.

Whether the Jesus of history actually foretold such an exaltation for himself is a difficult question, but Wright tellingly observes that "we do not find Daniel 7 used in this way, with this christological import, in early Christianity outside the reported words of Jesus".[23] Indeed, where the allusion to Daniel 7 turns up elsewhere in the New Testament (e.g., Acts 1:9–11; 1 Thess. 4:16–17) it has clearly been reinterpreted to refer to Christ's descent on the clouds at his anticipated return. Thus, Wright has offered a serious case for taking Mark 14:62 and parallels as an authentic—if scandalous—saying of Jesus.

This reference to other New Testament passages that anticipate a return of Christ does, however, move the discussion forward to a very important point: Wright's novel interpretation of the synoptic apocalyptic sayings *does not intend to negate or circumvent the church's expectation of a future return of Christ, resurrection of the dead, and final judgment.* Despite the fact that he thinks Jesus meant something else when he uttered the words that we now find in the synoptics, Wright does not want to debunk or demythologize future apocalyptic hope. Indeed, he acknowledges that elsewhere in the New Testament we do find an expectation of Christ's coming again. This point could easily escape readers of *Jesus and the Victory of God*, for it occupies no place in Wright's reconstruction of the historical Jesus; he mentions it only in passing.[24] Wright's position on this question is somewhat clearer in the first volume of his multivolume project, *The New Testament and the People of God*. Near the conclusion of that book, he discusses the hope of the early Christians and notes that they introduced several developments and innovations in relation to the Jewish eschatological tradition. One of these is, explicitly, "the expectation of the return of Jesus".[25] This expectation was a necessary innovation: "Precisely because Jesus' resurrection was the raising of one human being in the middle of the history of exile and misery, not the raising of all righteous human beings to bring the history of exile and misery to an end, there must be a further end yet in sight".[26] But Wright makes a careful distinction that must be observed in order to understand the theological import of the argument that he will make in his second volume: "It is vital to stress *both* that most of the texts normally drawn on in this connection [i.e., the return of Jesus] have nothing to do with the case, *and* that there are several others which still bear on it directly."[27] The only example of the latter category that Wright actually cites in this passage is Acts 1:10–11, but presumably he has in mind various Pauline texts as well. Thus, it would be a serious mistake to read Wright's historicizing interpretation of apocalyptic texts in *Jesus and the Victory of God* as a strategy for escaping the theological problems of unfulfilled apocalyptic hope.

Indeed, if anything, Wright's reading of the Jesus tradition cranks the tension between promise and present reality even higher; if Jesus has already enacted the return of YHWH to Zion, how can we possibly explain the persistence of suffering in the world? Wright sees this problem clearly and articulates it with characteristic eloquence: "Jesus interpreted his coming death, and the vindication he expected after that death, as the defeat of evil; but on the first Easter Monday evil still stalked the earth from Jerusalem to Gibralter and beyond, and stalks it still."[28] This means that, despite Wright's tendency to downplay the "delay of the parousia" as a problem for early Christian theology,[29] the urgency of our longing for final fulfillment can only be intensified by the foretaste of vindication that we have already been given. As Paul says,

> We know that the whole creation has been groaning in labor pains until now; and not only the creation, but we ourselves, who have the first fruits of the Spirit, groan inwardly while we wait for adoption, the redemption of our bodies (Rom. 8:22–23).

This theological problem—or, perhaps more accurately, this dimension of Christian experience—has not yet been adequately addressed by Wright's massive multivolume project, but it surely cries out to be dealt with in his future work.

III. Why We Need Apocalyptic Eschatology

We have surveyed three strategies for coping with the offense of the New Testament's apocalyptic theology: the Johannine tendency to envelop temporal eschatology in a timeless "vertical" eschatology of union with Christ; the revisionist dismissal of apocalyptic through isolating an idealized construction of Jesus from the canonical witnesses; and N. T. Wright's reading of the synoptic apocalyptic passages as symbolic references to events that have already occurred in the death and resurrection of Jesus. As we have seen, none of these strategies offers a satisfactory solution to the problem succinctly summarized by the author of the Letter to the Hebrews: "But now we do not yet see all things subjected to him" (Heb. 2:8). History continues its grinding litany of human atrocities, and we see no compelling evidence that God is answering the prayer that Jesus taught us to pray: "May your kingdom come; may your will be done on earth, as it is in heaven" (Matt. 6:10).

Consequently, as we begin a new millennium, the moment is propitious to recall that the preaching of the gospel—and the effort to comprehend theologically the gospel that we preach—cannot dispense with apocalyptic eschatology. The gospel is intelligible only within a narrative world shaped by biblical apocalyptic hope. Why is the New Testament's apocalyptic eschatology essential to Christian faith? The following enumeration of seven reasons is neither exhaustive nor fully developed, but it may serve as a starting place for further reflection.

(1) *The church needs apocalyptic eschatology to carry Israel's story forward.* Without a future-directed eschatological hope, we cannot affirm God's faithfulness to Israel, and the historical fate of the Jewish people becomes theologically unintelligible. The Old Testament repeatedly narrates God's promise of faithfulness to Israel, pointing towards a future day in which "the Lord will vindicate his people, have compassion on his servants" (Deut. 32:36). There will be a day, according to the prophetic promise, when God "will come to Zion as Redeemer" (Isa. 59:20) and gather the scattered exiles into a restored Israel where the glory of the Lord is manifest (Isa. 60:1–4), and the people neither suffer violence nor inflict it (Isa. 65:17–25). To be sure, the New Testament proclaims that these promises find their proleptic fulfillment in Jesus Christ and in the church as a prefiguration of the eschatological people of God, but the historical existence of the church is (only) a sign and anticipation of the full divine embracing (*proslēmpsis*) of the

eschatological Israel, including the empirical Jewish people who have—at least temporarily—refused the gospel (Rom. 11:15).

To put the matter differently, without apocalyptic eschatology, Christian theology becomes inescapably supersessionist. If we do not believe that God will ultimately fulfill his promises by restoring Israel, then the Old Testament can only be read in one of two ways: either it is merely an allegorical prefiguration of Christianity, or it is a primitive evolutionary stage now transcended by Christianity as a higher and purer religion. Either way, the outcome is a form of Christian theology that, when faced with Paul's plaintive question, "Has God rejected his people?", must answer, "Yes, as a matter of fact, he has." To give such an answer, however, is not only to reject Paul's anguished protestation to the contrary (Romans 9–11) but also to plunge our doctrine of God into an abyss of incoherence. If God can be faithless to Israel, then we are dealing with a fickle deity whose promises are not to be trusted.

God's apocalyptic deliverance of all Israel (Rom. 11:26–27) is the mysterious missing piece of the puzzle in God's sovereign dealings with the world. Such a future is necessary in order to make sense of the past.

(2) *The church needs apocalyptic eschatology for interpreting the cross as a saving event for the world.* A similar point can be made about the cross as the climax of Israel's story. If Christian preaching is "to know nothing ... except Jesus Christ and him crucified" (1 Cor. 2:2), we will find ourselves committed to telling an unfinished story, a story that requires an ending adumbrated, though not yet fully written, by the New Testament accounts of the resurrection. If we are to be faithful to the New Testament witnesses, we cannot interpret the death of Jesus solely as a propitiatory sacrifice for the forgiveness of the sins of individuals; the cross can be interpreted as an atoning event only when it is placed within the larger apocalyptic narrative of God's ultimate triumph over evil and death. In the event of the cross, God destroys the powers of the old order and inaugurates a new creation (Gal. 6:14–16); yet, the syntax of this narrative requires the eschatological reservation ("not yet") and the future orientation of hope. The point is elegantly illustrated by Paul's careful formulation in 1 Cor. 15:20–23, in which he insists that the resurrection of Jesus must be understood as the "first fruits" of the eschatological consummation:

> But in fact Christ *has been raised* from the dead, *the first fruits* of those who have died. For since death came through a human being, the resurrection of the dead *has* also *come* through a human being; for as all die in Adam, so all *will be* made alive in Christ. *But each in his own order: Christ the first fruits, then at his coming* (**en tē parousia autou**) *those who belong to Christ.*

Without this promise, whose final fulfillment we do not yet see, the cross can only be construed as a defeat rather than a victory over the world.

(3) *The church needs apocalyptic eschatology for the gospel's political critique of pagan culture.* Without the claim that Jesus is the one to whom, ultimately, every knee will bow and every tongue confess (Phil. 2:9–11), Christian theology loses its critical edge against pagan culture, accepts the politics of this world, and becomes spiritually otherworldly. "Render to Caesar the things that are Caesar's and to God the things that are God's" (Mark 12:17), rather than being heard in its original context as a challenge to apocalyptic discernment,[30] becomes domesticated into a maxim that cedes to Caesar sovereignty over the everyday world. But when we pray for the coming of the *basileia tou theou* on earth as it is in heaven, we continually reaffirm the politically subversive vocation of the church as an anticipation of God's future, and we anticipate the day when we can truly sing, "The kingdom of the world has become the kingdom of our Lord, and of his Christ" (Rev. 11:15). As Oliver O'Donovan has observed, the Apocalypse bears witness to "that authority of truth and righteousness which our experience of political society on earth has consistently denied us", thereby "confronting a false political order with the foundation of a true one".[31] It is, therefore, no accident that the book of Revelation comes hermeneutically into focus when it is read as a political resistance document by communities of oppressed people, as in the civil rights movement in the United States or the struggle against apartheid in South Africa.[32] Understood in this way, Revelation becomes a diagnostic tool that enables us to recognize that Caesar's power is transient —and thereby to resist the seductions of materialism and violence in the world around us.

The Magnificat of Mary (Luke 1:46–55), though its verbs are conjugated prophetically in the aorist tense, is a profoundly apocalyptic text, envisioning God's eschatological reversal of the fortunes of the powerful and the lowly, God's help for the hungry and dismissal of the rich. A church trained by such imagery to see God's new world coming can never lapse into comfortable accommodation with the status quo in an unjust world.

(4) *The church needs apocalyptic eschatology to resist ecclesial complacency and triumphalism.* I have just said that a church trained by apocalyptic imagery cannot lapse into accommodation with the status quo, but of course that is a prescriptive remark rather than a descriptive one. In fact, the church can and does lapse into complacency. Where this is so—as we are reminded by the lectionary texts each Advent season—apocalyptic eschatology sounds a wake-up call. Thus, the critical cutting edge of apocalyptic challenges not only pagan idolatry but also ecclesial self-satisfaction. The numerous synoptic parables warning servants to remain alert and faithful in the absence of their master (e.g. Matt. 24:45–25:30, placed significantly immediately following Matthew's "apocalypse" passage about the end of the age) stand as permanent reminders to the church in the time between the times that we must "be ready, for the Son of Man is coming at an unexpected hour" (Matt. 24:44; cf. Mark 13:32–37). How are we to be ready? "Blessed is that

slave whom his master will find at work when his master arrives" (Matt. 24:46).

The letters to the seven churches in Rev. 2:1–3:22 also illustrate this admonitory, corrective function of apocalyptic discourse. Words of comfort are spoken to communities that endure faithfully and keep God's word even though they have little power (e.g., Rev. 3:8), but the church at Laodicea, which perceives itself as rich and prosperous, is sternly warned of God's coming judgment: "because you are neither cold nor hot, I am about to spit you out of my mouth" (3:16–17). Those who heed Christ's prophetic warning, however, will be granted the final reward of exaltation with Christ on his throne (3:21). The looming reality of the final judgment serves to keep the church from grandiose perceptions of its own importance—for it is only a provisional servant of God's purposes in the time between the times—and also from becoming fat, sleepy, and abusive.[33]

(5) *The church needs apocalyptic eschatology in order to affirm the body.* This point may not be immediately obvious, because apocalyptic thought has so often been carelessly associated with "dualism" and annihilation of this-worldly reality. In fact, however, where Christian theology has remained most closely in touch with its Jewish apocalyptic roots, it has most firmly insisted on the value and importance of embodied existence, in contrast to forms of hellenized piety that regard the material realm as evil or inferior. The gospel proclaims the resurrection of the body, not the immortality of the disembodied soul. As Käsemann recognized, apocalyptic eschatology affirms the creator's final sovereignty over creation and his refusal to abandon it to decay. God is faithful to redeem what he has created. The alternative to the apocalyptic vision, then, is some form of Gnosticism that denies God's redemptive intention for creation and the body.

Paul had to drive this point home forcefully to some of the Corinthians who sought to accommodate the gospel to enlightened philosophical ideas about the transcendence of crass bodily existence. Paul insists, on the contrary, that the resurrection of the body is at the very heart of the gospel, and that those who deny it are lost in futility (1 Cor. 15:12–19). It may also follow that many of the Corinthians' moral problems were related to a perception that the body is of no consequence: sexual immorality (5:1–2, 6:12–20), rejection of sex within marriage (7:1–7), casual participation in eating idol meat (8:1–11:1), and excessive exaltation of certain spiritual gifts (12:1–14:40). Paul's final answer to these abuses is to reassert at great length the doctrine of the resurrection of the body (1 Corinthians 15), while taking care to explain that resurrection entails not merely an endorsement or continuation of embodied life as we know it but rather a transformation into a new embodied state beyond our limited powers of imagination (15:35–58).

Sadly, many Christians at the turn of the millennium have lost sight of the fundamental apocalyptic doctrine of the resurrection of the body. Those who continue to hope for some sort of post-mortem existence more often imagine a disembodied salvation of the soul. In this circumstance, theology may need a millennial reminder of Justin Martyr's fierce advocacy of the doctrine of the resurrection. He observes sourly that there are "some who are called Christians ... who say that there is no resurrection of the dead [*anastasis nekrōn*], and that their souls, when they die, are taken to heaven". He unhesitatingly labels such people as "godless, impious heretics", and declares that "I and others, who are right-minded Christians on all points, are assured that there will be a resurrection of the dead [*sarkos anastasin*]."[34] We may not need to emulate Justin's truculence, but the clarity of our theology would be well served by emulating his robust affirmation of the resurrection of the body.[35]

(6) *The church needs apocalyptic eschatology to ground its mission.* In Acts 1, at the conclusion of the risen Lord's instruction of apostles, they ask him, "Lord, is this the time when you will restore the kingdom to Israel?" (Acts 1:6). This is not a stupid question. Jesus has been teaching them about this very thing (1:4), and Luke has portrayed Jesus, from the beginning of his gospel, as one who will fulfill Israel's hope (e.g., Luke 1:54–55, 68–75). The raising of the crucified Jesus from the grave could easily be understood as an apocalyptic sign that the final restoration of Israel was indeed at hand. Jesus' answer, however, without rejecting the premise of their question, makes it clear that they are not to speculate about the timing of the kingdom's coming and that he has business for them to attend to: they are to be his witnesses in an expanding mission that will extend to the ends of the earth (Acts 1:7–8). These words of commissioning are Jesus' last words, for he is immediately taken up into heaven, before the eyes of the gaping apostles. Luke, in a deft narrative stroke, reinforces Jesus' message by bringing onstage two angelic figures who shatter the followers' reverie with a wry question and a piece of important information:

> "Men of Galilee, why do you stand looking up toward heaven? This Jesus, who has been taken up from you into heaven, will come in the same way as you saw him go into heaven" (1:11).

Just as Jesus did not reject the apostles' hope that perhaps the kingdom was at hand, so the angels reinforce the apocalyptic expectation of Jesus' coming again from heaven; just as Jesus redirected the apostles' attention away from speculation about the time of the restoration, so the angels implicitly redirect their attention from cloud-gazing to the words just spoken by Jesus. They say, in effect, "Why are you standing there gawking? You've been given a job to do!"

This interplay of apocalyptic expectation and missional imperative is programmatic for Luke's second volume. The coming of the Holy Spirit, which will empower the mission (1:8), is itself an eschatological sign of "the last days" (2:17, quoting Joel 2:28), and the apostles' work of testifying everywhere as Jesus' witnesses is therefore to be carried out as a fulfillment of eschatological prophecy about the extension of God's sovereignty over the whole world; the Spirit is now to be poured out on "all flesh" (2:17), and all who call on the name of the Lord will be saved (2:21, 39). Yet Luke consistently focuses attention not on speculative timetables and scenarios but on the formation of the church as an eschatological community manifesting God's grace and power (2:41–47; 4:32–37).

Without the apocalyptic outpouring of the Spirit, the formation of such a community is impossible. The community's identity is given in and with its commission to serve as the instrument of God's proclamation to the world; the "great grace" that is upon them—as attested by the eradication of poverty through their practices of economic sharing (4:32–35)—is a proleptic sign of the "universal restoration" promised by the prophets (3:21).

Thus, in this Lukan portrayal, the mission of the church develops under the umbrella of apocalyptic eschatology. Even while Luke creates an extended interval for the expansion of the mission throughout the empire, the mission itself makes sense only as a part of the unfolding plan of God, which is interpreted in apocalyptic categories: the apostles' preaching of the resurrection offers the possibilty of repentance in preparation for the day appointed for God's ultimate judgment (e.g., 17:31).

Luke is hardly alone among New Testament writers in depicting the mission of the church as the outworking of God's apocalyptic design for judgment and redemption of the world (see, e.g., 2 Cor. 5:11–6:2; Eph. 3:7–13). Precisely to the degree that Luke is perceived to downplay apocalyptic expectation, the observations offered here become the more striking: the mission of the church is comprehensible in Luke-Acts only as an endtime phenomenon. Without this theological grounding, the mission loses both its rationale and its urgency. It is perhaps not too much to suggest that the liberal Protestant church's loss of a sense of missional urgency is directly correlated with the evaporation of its eschatological expectation.

(7) *The church needs apocalyptic eschatology to speak with integrity about suffering and death.* The New Testament's vision of a final resurrection of the dead enables us to tell the truth about the present, including its tragedies and injustices, without sentimental sugar-coating, without cynicism or despair. It allows us to name suffering and death as real and evil, but not final.

Too often, Christians use pious language about how those who have died have "gone to heaven" or "have gone to a better place" in order to deny the reality of death. Worse, the denial of death sometimes completely trumps the teaching of Scripture and tradition; I recently listened with horror at a Christian memorial service as a well-meaning family member of the deceased read an overtly pantheistic poem, in which the speaking persona of the dead person claimed to be present in various natural phenomena of wind and stars and sunsets and so forth, concluding with the cruelly deceitful affirmation, "I did not die".

Against all of this, the New Testament's apocalyptic eschatology offers a sturdy realism that acknowledges the reality of death, while looking to God ultimately to restore life and set all things right. In 1 Thess. 4:13–18, Paul offers pastoral consolation concerning the deceased precisely by appealing to apocalyptic eschatology:

> But we do not want you to be uninformed, brothers and sisters, about those who have died, so that you may not grieve as others do who have no hope. For since we believe that Jesus died and rose again, even so, through Jesus, God will bring with him those who have died.

Paul continues his description of an apocalyptic scenario in which the Lord will descend from heaven with the sound of God's trumpet and the dead will rise and be caught up together with the living to be with the Lord forever. The striking thing is that Paul does not seek to comfort the grieving bereaved Thessalonians by telling them that their loved ones are already in heaven with Jesus. He acknowledges that the dead are dead and buried. The apocalyptic hope is that in the resurrection they will be reunited with the living in the new world brought into being at Christ's return. These are the words with which Christians are to "encourage one another" (1 Thess. 4:18). These same considerations apply on a larger scale to Christian theology's reflection about the terrible tragedies that violent human cultures bring upon the world. In the face of mass murders, non-apocalyptic theology is singularly trivial and helpless. As Dale Allison writes,

> … Jesus, the millenarian herald of judgment and salvation, says the only things worth saying … If our wounds never heal, if the outrageous spectacle of a history filled with cataclysmic sadness is never undone, if there is nothing more for those who were slaughtered in the death camps or for six-year olds devoured by cancer, then let us eat and drink, for tomorrow we die. If in the end there is no good God to calm this sea of troubles, to raise the dead, and to give good news to the poor, then this is indeed a tale told by an idiot, signifying nothing.[36]

But an apocalyptically formed Christian faith knows how to confess that, while we groan along with a creation in bondage to decay, we wait eagerly for the redemption of our bodies. We hope for what we do not see and trust that the glory that is to be revealed will swallow up death and mourning and pain, when, in the New Jerusalem, God will wipe away every tear from our eyes (Rom. 8:18–25; Rev. 21:1–4).

IV. The Hermeneutical Agenda: Apocalyptic Intratextuality

In the face of these formidable reasons why Christian theology requires apocalyptic eschatology, it might still be objected that some hermeneutical device is required to make apocalyptic thought intelligible for people in western culture at the dawn of this new millennium. Two objections in particular are often raised against the viability of apocalyptic theology.

First, hasn't the passage of time disconfirmed the literal apocalyptic hopes of the New Testament writers? The answer is, simply, no. The New Testament itself already makes clear that the duration of the present age is uncertain and the date of Christ's return unknowable to mortal kind. It is therefore foolish presumption for us to turn the calendar page and declare, "It's been too long now; I guess he's not coming." This complaint was being voiced already by "scoffers" at the time of the writing of 2 Peter, probably the latest document in the New Testament canon (2 Pet. 3:3–4). The answer given there (2 Pet. 3:8–10) is a theologically profound one, alluding to the Psalmist's doxological confession:

> For a thousand years in your sight
> are like yesterday when it is past,
> or like a watch in the night (Ps. 90:4).

Our mortal sense of temporality gives us no clue about God's timing, and we have no criteria to assess the appropriateness of the lag time between Christ's resurrection and *parousia*.

Second, hasn't science done away with the mythic cosmology presupposed by apocalyptic thought? This is where Wright's discussion of the character of apocalyptic language proves helpful.[37] As he rightly observes, such language was always poetic and metaphorical, from its Old Testament origins onwards. The imagery used to articulate the apocalyptic hope must be interpreted with literary discernment, not in a flat-footedly literal way. This is not a matter of demythologizing the text for modern readers but of interpreting the text in accordance with the literary conventions of its own time. For instance, when Mark's Gospel speaks of the sun and moon being darkened and the stars falling from the sky (Mark 13:24–25), these celestial portents should be read as figurative markers of cataclysmic *historical* events. Or again, Paul's poetic imagery of trumpets and clouds (1 Thess. 4:13–18) draws on the iconographic vocabulary of biblical apocalyptic to depict the firm future hope that God will not abandon his creation, that God will make all things new. The images refer to real events in the future (i.e., the return of Christ, the resurrection of the dead), but the details of the description are imaginative constructions that should not be pressed literalistically.

When the New Testament writers describe the shape of the eschatological reality, they often exercise noteworthy restraint, hinting at images seen through a glass darkly. Here, for example, is 1 John on the character of our transformed future existence: "Beloved, we are God's children now; what we will be has not yet been revealed. What we do know is this: when he is revealed, we will be like him, for we will see him as he is" (1 John 3:2). Or again, here is Paul on the character of the "glory that is to be revealed": "Now hope that is seen is not hope. For who hopes for what he sees? But if we hope for what we do not see, we wait for it with patient endurance" (Rom. 8:24–25). Such reverently restrained statements provide the interpretive lens through which we should read the more exuberant imagery of 1 Thessalonians 4 or the book of Revelation. Apocalyptic theology holds open the question of the shape of the redeemed world, rather than prematurely foreclosing it.

With these caveats in place, I would suggest that the difficulty of reading apocalyptic texts has been vastly overstated by interpreters who seek to minimize the apocalyptic content of Christian proclamation. In fact, given the centrality of apocalyptic thought in the New Testament and the failure of demythologizing hermeneutical strategies, Christian theologians should press forward to a robust recovery of apocalyptic teaching and preaching. This recommendation is not a marketing strategy calculated to exploit millennium fever, which will, in any case, already have abated by the time this article appears in print. The recovery of unabashed apocalyptic theology is, rather, a recommendation pressed upon us by the character of the New Testament witnesses themselves, who steadily and adamantly construe the significance of Jesus' proclamation, as well as his death and resurrection, within apocalyptic categories.

What aspects of the apocalyptic narrative are indispensible anchor points for us as we look to a future disclosure of God's redemptive purpose for the world? I would suggest that the New Testament's story leads us to affirm, in a strong literal sense,[38] the ultimate glorification of Jesus Christ as Lord over all creation, the resurrection of the body, God's final judgment of all humanity, and "the life of the world to come" in true justice and peace. The echo of the Nicene Creed in that formulation is no accident. The church's creedal heritage and its liturgy remind us again and again that the gospel is apocalyptic to the core. The Eucharistic liturgy condenses the gospel story into a threefold acclamation: "Christ has died, Christ is risen, Christ will come again." Any theology faithful to the New Testament witnesses must give balanced attention to all three moments of the story, two of which are indelibly apocalyptic in character.

What I am proposing here is an implication—not heretofore sufficiently noted—of George Lindbeck's salutary prescription that theology should be done as an "intratextual" enterprise.[39] If, as I have contended, the canonical New Testament is strongly apocalyptic in its interpretation of the story of Jesus, then to live and think within that story will necessarily draw the church into sharing its apocalyptic frame of reference. As we are formed by the story, we will learn to discern our own place as servants charged to watch expectantly in this time between the times.

NOTES

1   Raleigh *News and Observer*, May 16, 1999.
2   In 1991, Elisabeth Schüssler Fiorenza reported that Hal Lindsey's sensationalistic book, *The Late, Great Planet Earth* had sold *seven million* copies since its original publication in 1970 (*Revelation: Vision of a Just World* [Minneapolis, MN: Fortress Press, 1991], p. 8). It is a curious fact that sales figures for such books, sold primarily through chains of "Christian bookstores", are not included in the best seller lists of the *New York Times* and other "mainstream" media.
3   E. Käsemann, *New Testament Questions of Today* (Philadelphia, PA: Fortress Press, 1969), p. 137. Käsemann's fundamental insight on this point has been carried forward by the work of J. C. Beker and J. L. Martyn, both of whom should be counted among the influences for the position that I develop in this essay.
4   R. Bultmann, *The Gospel of John* (Philadelphia, PA: Westminster Press, 1971), pp. 11, 219–220, pp. 261–262.
5   In his *Theology of the New Testament*, vol. 2 (New York, NY: Scribner, 1955), p. 85, Bultmann also suggested that the same ecclesiastical editor responsible for the apocalyptic insertions in the Fourth Gospel might have added these passages as well.
6   R. E. Brown, *The Community of the Beloved Disciple* (New York, NY: Paulist Press, 1979), pp. 93–144.
7   See particularly *Theology of the New Testament*, vol. 2, pp. 75–92: "Faith as Eschatological Existence". On p. 85, Bultmann writes, "John has abandoned the old conception of Jesus' parousia held by the earliest church. The 'world' will see nothing of his coming again."
8   R. W. Funk, "The Issue of Jesus", *Forum* 1/1 (1985) pp. 7–12.
9   R. W. Funk, R. W. Hoover, *et al.*, *The Five Gospels: The Search for the Authentic Words of Jesus* (New York, NY: Macmillan, 1993), p. 137.
10   Ibid., p. 4; cf. p. 137.
11   M. Borg, *Jesus: A New Vision* (San Francisco, CA: Harper & Row, 1987), p. 14. Borg explains in a footnote (p. 20, n. 25) that this claim is based on a mail poll of members of the Jesus Seminar and participants in the Historical Jesus Section of the Society of Biblical Literature. The actual data are provided in his subsequent book, *Jesus in Contemporary Scholarship* (Valley Forge, PA: Trinity Press International, 1994), pp. 59–60: the poll received 39 responses from the membership of these two groups, 23 of whom answered that they did not think Jesus "expected the end of the world in his generation". Considering that the Society of Biblical Literature has several thousand members, readers may draw their own conclusions about the validity of this poll's sampling method. Perhaps even more crucial, however, is the wording of the question: the key phrase is "the end of the world". Although I would strongly maintain that Jesus was an apocalyptic prophet, I do not think he expected "the end of the world". What he expected was the resurrection of the dead and God's righteous final judgment. Thus, the wording of Borg's question blurs the issue. It should be noted, however, that *Jesus in Contemporary Scholarship* contains a helpful essay, "Jesus and Eschatology: Current Reflections" (pp. 69–96) in which Borg significantly qualifies his claims: he admits that "Jesus probably had some eschatological beliefs", that "Jesus was concerned about the future", and that Jesus "speaks in a time of crisis, issues indignant indictments of ruling elites, and warns passionately of coming catastrophe" (pp. 88–89). These clarifications bring Borg's picture of Jesus into closer proximity with the position I am advocating in the present essay.
12   In addition to Borg's work, see particularly B. Mack, *A Myth of Innocence: Mark and Christian Origins* (Philadelphia, PA: Fortress Press, 1988); J. D. Crossan, *The Historical Jesus: The Life of a Mediterranean Jewish Peasant* (San Francisco, CA: HarperSanFrancisco, 1991).
13   E. P. Sanders, *Jesus and Judaism* (Philadelphia, PA: Fortress Press, 1985), pp. 91–95.
14   Borg, *Jesus in Contemporary Scholarship*, pp. 76–80.
15   D. C. Allison, *Jesus of Nazareth: Millenarian Prophet* (Minneapolis, MN: Fortress Press, 1998).
16   Here again, Borg is a partial exception. His dichotomy between the "pre-Easter Jesus" and the "post-Easter Jesus" allows him to maintain a constructive place for the "Christ of faith" in his overall perspective.
17   N. T. Wright, *Jesus and the Victory of God* (Minneapolis, MN: Fortress Press, 1996), p. 77.
18   Ibid., pp. 339–368.

19   See his chapter, "The Return of the King", ibid., pp. 612–653.
20   Ibid., pp. 642–644.
21   See the collection of responses to Wright's work in C. Newman (ed), *Jesus and the Restoration of Israel: A Critical Assessment of N. T. Wright's "Jesus and the Victory of God"* (Downers Grove, IL: InterVarsity Press, forthcoming).
22   See N. T. Wright, *The New Testament and the People of God* (Minneapolis, MN: Fortress Press, 1991), pp. 291–297.
23   Wright, *Jesus and the Victory of God*, p. 644.
24   E.g., ibid., p. 635.
25   Wright, *The New Testament and the People of God*, p. 461.
26   Ibid., p. 459.
27   Ibid., p. 461.
28   Wright, *Jesus and the Victory of God*, p. 659.
29   E.g., Wright, *The New Testament and the People of God*, pp. 462–464.
30   C. Myers, *Binding the Strong Man: A Political Reading of Mark's Story of Jesus* (Maryknoll, NY: Orbis Books, 1988), p. 312.
31   O. O'Donovan, "The Political Thought of the Book of Revelation", *Tyndale Bulletin* 37 (1986) p. 90.
32   Elizabeth Schüssler Fiorenza, *Revelation*; R. B. Hays, *The Moral Vision of the New Testament* (San Francisco, CA: HarperSanFrancisco, 1996), pp. 181–184.
33   For a treatment of the pastoral functions of apocalyptic judgment language, see the excellent study by David Kuck, *Judgment and Community Conflict: Paul's Use of Apocalyptic Judgment Language in 1 Corinthians 3:5–4:5* (NovTSup 66; Leiden: Brill, 1992).
34   *Dialogue with Trypho*, 80.
35   For further discussion, see R. B. Hays, *First Corinthians* (Interpretation Commentaries; Louisville, KY: John Knox Press, 1997), pp. 252–282.
36   Allison, *Millenarian Prophet*, p. 219.
37   Wright, *The New Testament and the People of God*, pp. 280–338. See also G. B. Caird, *The Language and Imagery of the Bible* (London: Duckworth, 1980).
38   On the meaning of "literal sense", see K. Greene-McCreight, *Ad Litteram: How Augustine, Calvin, and Barth Read the "Plain Sense" of Genesis 1–3* (Issues in Systematic Theology 5; New York, NY: Peter Lang, 1999).
39   G. Lindbeck, *The Nature of Doctrine: Religion and Theology in a Postliberal Age* (Philadelphia, PA: Westminster Press, 1984), pp. 112–138. Lindbeck writes, "Intratextual theology redescribes reality within the scriptural framework rather than translating Scripture into extrascriptural categories. It is the text, so to speak, which absorbs the world, rather than the world the text" (p. 118).

INDEX

Note: Page references in brackets indicate allusion or disguised reference.

Printed and bound by CPI Group (UK) Ltd, Croydon, CR0 4YY

13/04/2025

14656562-0004